How to Forgive When You Don't Feel Like It!

How to Forgive When You Don't Feel Like It!

by Joy Haney

New Leaf Press

First printing: February 1996

Copyright © 1995 by New Leaf Press. All rights re-
served. Printed in the United States of America. No
part of this book may be used or reproduced in any
manner whatsoever without written permission of the
publisher except in the case of brief quotations in
articles and reviews. For information write: New Leaf
Press, Inc., P.O. Box 311, Green Forest, AR 72638.

ISBN: 0-89221-322-1
Library of Congress Catalog Number: 93:084460

Dedication

With love and honor I dedicate this book to:

My beloved husband, Kenneth Haney;
My dear children:
    Sherrie and Glen Woodward,
    Nathaniel and Kim Haney,
    Elizabeth and John Shivers,
    Stephanie Haney,
    Angela Haney;
To my grandchildren:
    Mychail, and Elizabeth's unborn child.

May you always keep your face toward the sun and may the Son of Righteousness shine upon you. Let wonder and love stay alive in your heart as you walk life's pathways. Do not settle in ease and comfort, but dare and endure. As a gem cannot be polished without friction, neither will your life be without trials. As you encounter life's storms and struggles, retain hope, integrity, and purpose; for you were born to win and excel.

Table of Contents

PREFACE

If your life has been charred and blackened by the hot fires of hurt and the searing flames of injustice, this book is for you. Read it with an open searching heart, apply the principles, and you will live and build again. No night ever lasted forever. The following quote and poem are from the book, *Quests and Conquests*, compiled by Dean Dutten, written over 70 years ago.

> I am bigger than anything that can happen to me. All these things, sorrow, misfortune, and suffering, are outside the door. I am in the house and I have the key.

> Not until each loom is silent
> And the shuttles cease to fly,
> Will God unroll the pattern
> And explain the reason why
> The dark threads are as needful
> In the Weaver's skillful hand,
> As the threads of gold and silver
> For the pattern which He planned.[1]

Sometimes things do not go the way He planned because of stubborn human will. Judas proved this. Life does not always go the way you plan either, but

dancing on top of your hurt

you can use your hurtful experiences as <u>stepping stones instead of stumbling stones</u>. They can become learning experiences that will enrich your life and the lives of others if you will allow them to be.

Remember, you can be branded by the hate generated by the destructive fire, and your life can be filled with ashes, or you can be beautified by choosing to forgive, even those who do not deserve forgiveness. This book will help you clean out the cold bitter ashes of despair, and can cause you to dance on top of your hurt. It will help you look up to the stars of hope instead of down at the flames of bitter defeat. You can live again with happiness, peace, and joy.

— Joy Haney

*Stepping Stones
not Stumbling blocks*

1

THE ENEMY'S FIRE

The young man lay charred, scorched, and blistered on the hospital bed, unable to move or talk because of the pain and extensive burns he had suffered. The inferno from which he had escaped was the wreck of an airplane. The torment of the fiery holocaust was indeed enough, but now he suffered with internal anguish, also. His fiancée had just walked into the room and placed her engagement ring between his toes without saying a word. As he lay upon his bed, seemingly with his future obliterated, all he could do was cry silently while tears ran down the blackened sides of his face.

You probably will not go through the physical suffering this young man endured, but if you live long enough you will be "burnt" by someone or a situation involving other people. When you look around, you see many people who get burnt daily. The high society Trump family had its very public burning. Even the bums in the gutter have their hurtful moments. Everyone, sooner or later, will feel the hot fires of humiliation, hurts, and the searing flame of injustice.

From the beginning of time, people have been burned and devastated because of disappointing and marred relationships. This includes inventors who were mocked and ostracized by "normal" society, and musicians who were not respected until many years after their death. Our very own President Abraham Lincoln was the target of much verbal abuse when he endeavored to free the slaves.

Biblical figures who were burned include Joseph, whose brothers rejected him; as well as David who was hated and persecuted by Saul. Judas burnt Jesus by betrayal. Steven tried to help people, but they did not understand him. The very ones he tried to help "burned" him by stoning him. Haman tried to burn Mordecai, and in doing so got burned himself. Abel was burnt by Cain, Hagar by Sarah, and Samson by Delilah.

Job was burnt by Satan. He was a very wealthy man in Bible days who lived in the land of Uz. He became involved in a contest that developed between God and Satan. He had sevens sons and three daughters and was considered to be the greatest man of the East.

All his riches did not keep Satan from trying to destroy him. God was having a meeting with the sons of God and Satan came also among them. "And the Lord said unto Satan, Whence comest thou? Then Satan answered the Lord, and said, From going to and fro in the earth, and from walking up and down in it. And the Lord said unto Satan, Hast thou considered my servant Job, that there is none like him in the earth?" (Job 1:7-8).

Can you imagine God and Satan talking about a man on the earth like that? They talked back and forth until Satan told God that Job only served Him because of all his riches. Satan then told God to put forth His hand and touch all that he had and Job would curse God. So God answered Satan with confidence by saying, "Behold, all that he hath is in thy power; only upon himself put not forth thine hand. So Satan went forth from the presence of the Lord" (Job 1:12).

Notice, God gave Satan power to work against Job. One of the things Satan used to try to hurt Job with was fire. "While he was yet speaking, there came also another, and said, The fire of God is fallen from heaven, and hath burned up the sheep, and the servants, and consumed them; and I only am escaped alone to tell thee" (Job 1:16).

The servant, not knowing of the conversation between God and the devil, called the fire that destroyed them the fire of God. God did not send the fire. He gave Satan the power to use the elements against Job. John 10:10 says, "The thief cometh not, but for to steal, and to kill, and to destroy: I am come that they might have life, and that they might have it more abundantly." Satan, who is the enemy of mankind, always comes to destroy. Every chance he can get he will try to break up marriages, bring depression, and cause rebellion in children. He only wants to kill, steal, and destroy. His fire always burns, demolishes, and consumes.

He plans his strategy well. He constantly looks for ways to make people as miserable as he is. He who was once the leader of music in heaven is now the leader of misery. He who lost his song is now the director of sorrow, tears, and agony.

He becomes like a black widow spider, weaving a web to ensnare all who are unaware of his presence. When he lures the unexpected into his trap, he then injects his poisonous substance. The poison flows

Satan wants you to be as miserable as he is

through the mind developing into a searing, red-hot fire of destruction burning all things in its pathway. He loves to destroy relationships.

The enemy's destructive fire can be likened also to the ant-lion. The ant-lion is a little dark-looking creature that makes a conical hole in the sand, and puts itself in the very center. It then buries itself completely out of sight except its jaws, which appear like a rusty needle waiting for its victim.

From time to time a little ant comes along seeking her food in her usual busy way. She will see the rim of the sandy hump and peer over to investigate. As she senses danger she will try to rush away, but it is always too late. The sand will roll from under her feet and cause her to go down to the bottom. It is then the jaws open like a pair of shears and clips off a leg. Every time the ant tries to get out the jaws of the ant-lion keep clipping until finally, all the ant's legs are gone.

The ant-lion stays hidden the whole time until the ant gives up the struggle and the lion devours her. Then, with a flip of his tail, he throws the skin of the ant entirely out of the cup, and the trap is set for another victim.

That is the business of the enemy and his helpers. The good part of this story is that you are not helpless like the little red ant. Even though she tried to get out and was unable to, you are able to rise above the pit of despair that your burning caused you to sink into.

Fire has been a destructive force down through the ages. Thousands of acres of trees have been destroyed because of it. Homes, cities, automobiles, and countless lives are blackened and done away with because of fire. Blazing infernos caused by war bombs have destroyed the peace of nations, leaving in their aftermath ruin and rage.

The ashes of life that the first seven chapters of this book deal with relate to circumstances and relationships. The fires of anger, distrust, unfaithfulness, and rebellion can burn themselves deep into the heart and mind of those involved, causing great harm. The person that experiences a burning always feels the scalding scorch of blistering words and irate tempers.

The enemy's fire is no respecter of persons. It rains on the just and the unjust. It comes unwelcomed and uninvited. Sometimes it comes when it is least expected. You are like the little ant, going about your business, when suddenly the earth of circumstances opens and you fall headlong into it. It is not on your schedule. You did not plan on it; it just came. You did not invite it. You were not even aware it was on its way. It just dropped in like a fiery bombshell exploding on top of your head, seemingly blowing your world apart.

It is like the story about a flock of hens at feeding time. They were all eating their corn when suddenly one hen began fluttering about wildly. She seemed to be attempting to swallow a large lizard. The other hens were gathering around her cackling loudly, also.

It was discovered that while the hen had evidently pecked at the lizard, the slimy, twisting creature had turned about and had the hen by the throat and would have choked her to death had not the observers intervened.

The very people with whom you are involved can at some point turn on you and grab you by the throat, as happened to the hen, with words or action that can cause you to feel like the very breath has been knocked out of you. This happened to Joseph in his association with his brothers. He did them no wrong, just excited jealousy in them, until they turned on him and tried to destroy him.

Life sometimes will extend to you a hurtful experience. You will try to be brave, swallow your pride, and hold your head up without showing your hurt. Many times it becomes too big for you to handle.

Tears become your partner. Your heart is in perpetual pain as if a knife was taking up residence there. You search your heart, mind, and soul for the answers, and yet the answers seem to mock you. The things that were familiar have now become strangers to you. Your world is turned upside-down by the ugliness of a relationship that has gone sour. Where once there was happiness and laughter, now there is sorrow and pain. How did it all happen? When did it all begin? Who was to blame? Could it have been avoided if things had been done differently? You search for answers that seem to hide behind corners. Solutions become evasive and tears expose the pain in your heart. As you look back at the experience you feel as if all is hopeless.

The story of the Portuguese coastal steamer explains how you feel. There were fifty-three crewmen, three hundred Portuguese troops, and two hundred Mozambique Africans aboard when they became grounded on a sandbar off East Africa during a storm. While rescue efforts were being made from the shore, fire broke out on the ship. The fire spread to the stores of ammunition and the whole ship exploded in flames. Many of the passengers jumped into the sea — only to be attacked by sharks. Those who did manage to make the shore were threatened by lions roaring in a nearby jungle.

You feel like the passengers on the boat. First the storm, then the fire, the explosion, the sharks, and the lions. You feel like you cannot win for losing, *yet no one can make you lose but yourself.* No man can put you down for a long period of time. Prisons, fires, broken relationships, and death cannot destroy your spirit, but you have to work at it. It is not easy to restore things that are lost, but it is possible to begin again without the ashes of bitterness in your mouth.

Henry W. Longfellow said it well in his poem, "Psalm of Life."

> Tell me not in mournful numbers,
> "Life is but an empty dream!"
> For the soul is dead that slumbers
> And things are not what they seem.
>
> Life is real! Life is earnest!
> And the grave is not its goal,
> "Dust thou art, to dust returnest,"
> Was not spoken of the soul.
>
> Not enjoyment, and not sorrow,
> Is our destined end or way;
> But to act, that each tomorrow
> Finds us farther than today.
>
> Art is long, and time is fleeting,
> And our hearts, tho stout and brave,
> Still like muffled drums, are beating
> Funeral marches to the grave.
>
> In the world's broad field of battle,
> In the bivouac of life,
> Be not like dumb, driven cattle!
> Be a hero in the strife!
>
> Trust no future, howe'er pleasant!
> Let the dead past bury its dead!
> Act — act in the living present!
> Heart within and God o'erhead.

Lives of great men all remind us
We can make our lives sublime,
And, departing leave behind us
Footprints on the sands of time.

Footprints, that perhaps another,
Sailing o'er life's solemn main,
A forlorn and shipwrecked brother
Seeing, shall take heart again.

Let us then, be up and doing,
With a heart for any fate,
Still achieving, still pursuing,
Learn to labor and to wait.[1]

When the fire comes, determine in your heart that you are not going to let it destroy you. You will fight and win because you are not alone. Matthew Henry said, "Man's extremity is God's opportunity. Extremities are a warrant for importunities. A man at his wit's end is not at his faith's end."[2] The enemy cannot win against God. He never has and he never will. After the death of Jesus, where was the first place He went? He went to the enemy and demanded of him the keys to death. The grave could not keep Him. He said, "I am he that liveth, and was dead; and, behold, I am alive forevermore, Amen; and have the keys of hell and of death" (Rev. 1:18). Remember when you get burnt this is the kind of power you have on your side.

"at it's End and Fault
Beginning"

2

BURNT!

She sat in my office, a broken woman, tears running down her face, relating the details of the situation in which she had been burned. The person that "burnt" her was her husband, the one who professed to love her. She looked at me with despair in her eyes and I heard the despair in her voice. I sensed the icy fingers of desperation that gripped her soul and plunged her mind into an abyss of hell.

Her hell included abuse, disregard for her feelings, and a pattern of unfaithfulness by a man who was perverted in his thoughts and actions. He professed to know God, but did not show God to others. The wounds from the fire of her "hell" were infected, bleeding, and extremely painful.

Her world was one of degradation, humiliation, and hopelessness. Questions swirled in her brain like muddy flood waters sweeping down all consciousness of hope and life. Was there to be evil forever? Where could she turn? What could she do? What was to become of her and her children?

Anger, hurt, and disillusionment poured out of

her like blackened volcanic lava. Her bitter outcry filled the room with sounds of discord and ricocheted off the walls with the force of dynamite. The pretty dark-haired lady who looked so refined had been seared with the hot iron of her husband's sins. She and her children bore the brand of his selfishness. This was the real world for those who disregarded the laws of God.

You may also bear the scars of life's hurtful experiences. You may even be the picture of culture, leading a disciplined life, but seething down deep with the details of a situation where you got "burnt." Almost everyone in life will encounter hurtful situations where they feel like they have been burnt.

I watched another refined and beautiful lady walk through the fires of an unexpected divorce seemingly for no real reason at all. Her life was all together when suddenly her husband decided he wanted to marry a younger woman. She moved from her well-established home to a smaller house. She went through the process of shock, grief, anger, and disillusionment. She had seemed to be the perfect wife. No one could explain it, no one could believe it, and yet she had been burnt. Her secure world had been shattered by the raging fires of lust.

There are many ways in which the destructive fire of life can burn you. All situations where there are deep burns involve human relationships:

a. children against parents
b. parents against children
c. husbands against wives
d. wives against husbands
e. other family members against one another: uncles, aunts, grandparents, nieces, cousins, etc.

f. employer against employee
g. employee against employer
h. business associate against partner
i. business deals involving different per-
   sonalities
j. nation against nation
k. people against leadership
l. friends against friends
m. political foes against one another

The list is endless. All homes, churches, and busi-
nesses would be cold without the warmth of human
relationships. The fire of love can build, whereas the
fire of hatred can burn. The fire of lust can hurt,
whereas the fire of compassion can build up. Human
souls on fire with inspiration can build or destroy.
Hitler was on fire with an idea but destroyed many
lives, whereas Abraham Lincoln was on fire with an
idea, and fought for the cause of freedom for all slaves.

Humans turn houses into homes or hells. They
make the town square friendly or cold. People's attitudes, emotions, feelings, and deep-seated vibrations
spill over into the churches, communities, and market
places. When there are five billion people living together in a world that is influenced by those who tend
to be negative in their outlook, many of the people will
be "burnt."

Physical burns are painful injuries which may
prove fatal if severe enough, or if they cover a large
area. Burns may be caused not only by fire, but by hot
metals, chemicals, radiation, or electricity.

The classification of burns is determined by the
depth of the tissue injury. First-degree burns are those
in which the surface is red and painful, but the skin is
not broken or blistered. Second-degree burns are those

in which blisters are formed. Third-degree burns are deep, with charring and actual destruction of the skin and tissue. Second- and third-degree burns frequently become infected and are very serious.

Those who treat the patient must consider the possibility of severe shock caused by the extreme pain of second- and third-degree burns. These health care professionals must work rapidly so the patient does not become chilled, which can lead to shivering and then pneumonia.

The same care and consideration has to be taken with an emotionally burned patient. Wounds can become infected with bitterness, grudges, and resentments. Poison can ooze from the spirit, mind, and soul. The burn can be so deep that the wound takes time to heal. Just as a burn patient has to guard against the chill factor, so does the emotionally burned patient. The shock of the burn can chill the mind, soul, and spirit with cold hatred. When hate takes up residence in the soul of the emotionally burned patient, it controls his life with a scepter of revenge and hard, calloused emotions. His feelings become icicle brittle, with little compassion.

The emotional tissues of the heart that are destroyed by the insensitivity of the one who burned them are replaced by iron bands instead of tender strings. The weeping of this hurt becomes a cry of rage instead of the expression of a warm and caring heart. The personality becomes a hard shell where once there were special qualities of tenderness. People who experience the shock of an emotional hurt or burn tend to erect barriers and walls to keep out any further danger of being hurt. Instead of being open and vulnerable, they become guarded and hardened.

Instead of thinking great thoughts and moving

ahead, they become bogged down, their minds churning over and over with ways to get even. The object of their thoughts is the people who hurt them. Their soul is eaten up with the injustice of the past. It haunts their thoughts day and night. It whispers to them in their bed at night and follows them like a shadow even on the sunniest day. It actually moves in and dominates all waking thoughts and even troubles them in their dreams from time to time. Life in the day and life in the night become a nightmare.

Terror fills their mind over what has happened and the cry is always there, *Maybe, "if" I would have done this, it would not have happened.* Or, *"if" I would have done that, maybe I could have stopped it. If, if, if; but now it seems to be all over.*

This is where hope must enter the door. In a cellar in Cologne, Germany after World War II, these words were found on the wall:

I BELIEVE . . .
I believe in the sun,
    even when it is not shining.
I believe in love,
    even when I feel it not.
I believe in God,
    even when He is silent.

It is not a curse to go through rough times. It is a curse to let them cause you to die inside.

Many years ago a young midwestern lawyer suffered such deep depression that his friends thought it wise to keep all knives and razors from him. During this time he wrote, "I am now the most miserable man

living. Whether I shall ever be better, I cannot
tell. I awfully forbode I shall not." He was
wrong. He did recover and went on to become one of America's most loved presi-
dents, Abraham Lincoln.[1]

You may think that you will never make it, but
you will. You must hang onto hope in the midst of the
fire, and hope will put an asbestos suit around you. It
will bring you through wearing battle scars, but leave
your spirit unscathed by detrimental forces. When
you are weak, that is when Jesus becomes strong in
your life. He will walk with you through the fire just as
He did with the three Hebrew children.

The three young men were Shadrach, Meshach,
and Abednego. They had been captured and carried
away from Jerusalem to Babylon under the rule of
King Nebuchadnezzar. Several years later he had a
great image of gold made, the height of which was
threescore cubits, and the breadth six cubits. He called
a great meeting of all the people and ordered everyone
to fall down at the sound of the music and worship the
image. If anyone failed to obey the king's commandment they would be cast into the midst of a burning
fiery furnace.

The music played and everyone bowed down
low to the ground except the three Hebrew men. This
enraged the king and he called them forward. He told
them one more time that if they did not bow down at
the sound of music the second time, they would surely
burn. He even mocked them by saying, "Who is that
God that shall deliver you out of my hands?"

They answered respectfully, "We are not careful
to answer thee in this matter. If it be so, our God whom
we serve is able to deliver us from the burning fiery

furnace, and he will deliver us out of thine hand, O king. But if not, be it known unto thee, O king, that we will not serve thy god, nor worship the golden image which thou hast set up."

The fury of the king was so great that he ordered the furnace to be heated seven times hotter than it was. The three young men were bound in their coats, hats, and other garments and thrown into the fiery furnace. The flame of the fire slew the men that threw them in, but a miracle took place inside the furnace.

White-faced with astonishment the king asked the question as he peered inside, "Did not we cast three men bound into the midst of the fire?"

They answered and said unto the king, "True, O King."

He answered and said, "Lo, I see four men loose, walking in the midst of the fire, and they have no hurt; and the form of the fourth is like the Son of God." Then Nebuchadnezzar came near to the mouth of the burning fiery furnace, and spoke, and said, "Shadrach, Meshach, and Abednego, ye servants of the most high God, come forth, and come hither."

Then Shadrach, Meshach, and Abednego came out of the midst of the fire. And the princes, governors, captains, and the king's counselors, being gathered together, saw these men, upon whose bodies the fire had no power, nor was a hair of their head singed, their coats were not changed, and the smell of fire had not passed on to them.

The three did not choose their station in life, they did not choose to be captured, neither did they choose to go into a fiery furnace. The conviction of their hearts toward their God caused them to be threatened, taunted, and mocked. They became a spectacle not of their own choosing, but because of the anger of someone else. They became the brunt of another's pride and anger. (See Daniel 3:15-27.)

The Word of God instructs that offenses, hurts, and tribulations will come. You will walk through the fire, but the question is: What will you do once you come out of the fire? Will you be bitter or will you choose to worship God as you look at the pile of ashes? When you are going through excruciating pain it is difficult to believe that what you are experiencing is able to make you richer, wiser, and more fruitful.

> Out of the presses of pain,
> Cometh the soul's best wine;
> And the eyes that have shed no rain,
> Can shed but little shine.
> — M.R. DeHaan[2]

3

BUILDING SHRINES FROM ASHES

The fire is out, the coals are extinguished, and the house seems quiet and cold. The warmth is gone; only stark dead ashes remain. Ashes are what you have left after everything is consumed. An interesting passage of Scripture in Isaiah talks about idolatry and ashes. "Yea, he maketh a god, and worshippeth it; he maketh it a graven image, and falleth down thereto . . . . And the residue thereof he maketh a god, even his graven image: he falleth down unto it, and worshippeth it, and prayeth unto it . . . . He feedeth on ashes" (Isa. 44:14-20).

This passage shows the absurd reasoning of man. He will take a tree, make a fire, roast meat, warm himself, and bake bread with it. From the same tree he will make a god and bow down and worship it. The god will burn and all that will be left is ashes. It is the same way today. Someone will try to make a god out of things that are totally the opposite of God. The thing they become a slave to cannot help them, but it will destroy them. People make shrines out of the ashes or leftovers of a hurtful situation.

When you are burned by someone the first inclination of the human mind is to play over and over all the events that led up to the burning. You condemn yourself further by rationalizing, *Maybe IF I would have done so and so, this would never have happened. IF I would just have not done this and IF I would have done that, this probably would not have happened.* It goes on and on endlessly. You continually rehearse it in your mind until it is memorized. These thoughts become the thing you give your allegiance to constantly.

Your mind is consumed day and night with the ifs, whys, and how comes. Anything you give your allegiance to more than God becomes your god. From the ashes you are tempted to build a shrine to the wrong things. Despair, bitterness, resentments, grudges, loneliness, hate, and unforgiveness sometimes become your soul-mate. You counsel with your own thoughts, often leaving out the counsel of the Scripture.

Oftentimes the hurt is so deep that you do not want to give up the resentment. You want to hate the offending person because of what he or she did to you. You feel that by hating them you are getting even with them. It becomes a heavy weight in your heart. A big stone is placed in your path to victory. It is impossible to have victory as long as that stone is there.

There was once a king who ruled over a kingdom in which he watched the people grow more and more unkind and selfish. Thinking to himself that he would teach them a lesson he put a large stone in the middle of the thoroughfare. Under the stone he placed a bag of gold that was hidden from view.

He watched day after day as the people would drive their carriages around the stone instead of removing the stone. One day as the king rode down the thoroughfare, he came to the stone and stopped his carriage. All the people watched the king as he stepped down from the carriage and removed the large stone himself.

To their surprise, he then lifted the bag of gold and read the message inside the sack. It simply said, "This bag of gold belongs to the soul who took the time to make the road a little easier for his fellow man to travel." All the people were bitterly disappointed, but learned a hard lesson that day.

Sometimes, the ashes bank together and become heavy like a stone. It may look small, but the weight of it brings a heaviness into your whole system. Laughter goes, enthusiasm is dampened, and instead of worshipping at the altar of God, you now worship at the shrine of worry, hurt, and disillusionment.

The dust from the ashes swirl up into your eyes and you become spiritually deceived. The taste of ashes gets in your mouth. "He feedeth on ashes: a deceived heart hath turned him aside" (Isa. 44:20). You eat them for breakfast, lunch, and dinner. The hurt accompanies you to the table, grocery store, job, and even to church. It swirls in your nostrils and mouth as dust from a dust storm. The ashes blind you and you become deceived, bowing down in your heart to the shrine that now has become your god. You not only eat the ashes of it, but it eats at you. It is like a jackhammer in your brain pounding daily into your consciousness and subconscious mind the hurts, reasons, and aftermath of the burning. The jackhammer gets so loud sometimes that you want to cover up your ears. Even when you cover up your ears you still hear it because it is boring deeper and deeper into your spirit. The hurt becomes a permanent resident instead of the visitor that comes through each of our lives at one time or another. The hurt literally moves in and sets up a stronghold in the hole the jackhammer of hate and resentment bore.

After it becomes a stronghold, there must be victuals brought into the stronghold to keep it fortified. "And he fortified the strongholds, and put captains in them and store of victual" (2 Chron. 11:11).

A stronghold is a place of security, a fort, or a place of fortified strength. You become secure with your stronghold because it is a blanket or a cushion against progress. You settle down into a hole and lie there wounded, hoping the pain will go away.

Your mind is like a city. It has gates and strongholds just like the cities of old. They had fortresses, or strongholds, where captains were placed to guard the city. Strongholds determine who goes in and out of the city. If the wrong man gets in the stronghold, the city is in trouble, because he will let the enemy inside.

The captains of fear, disillusionment, anger, self-pity, and hopelessness can dominate you until the walls are broken down into a deplorable state of mind. The victuals, or food for thought, continue to feed the captains until they become more and more powerful.

Circumstances and your thoughts can drag you down to the ash heap. The Scripture paints a graphic picture of this happening to Job, "And he sat down among the ashes" (Job 2:8). Ephesians 6:13 says "to stand and having done all, just stand." Job could not stand his situation any longer. He just sat down, mourned, and asked questions while his friends accused him falsely.

His life was seemingly destroyed. He had nothing left but a pile of ashes and a wife who had lost faith. It is so easy to give up, sit down, and mourn when devastation descends upon you. Who feels like singing, running, or even standing when there is deep pain? It is not difficult to have bitter thoughts. It is natural to accuse, threaten, and harbor ill will.

This is when shrines are erected. There is just cause for hurt and bitterness, so why not bow down to it and give in to the searing pain? "The hurt is so deep, why does it matter what I do anyway?" you ask. "Everything good is destroyed. Why fight against it? It is easier to bow down under the pressure than to rise up and start over," you reason.

The cry of the one who is "burnt" is well-described in Psalm 102:1-9,11. "Hear my prayer, O Lord, and let my cry come unto thee. Hide not thy face from me in the day when I am in trouble; incline thine ear unto me: in the day when I call answer me speedily. For my days are consumed like smoke, and my bones are burned as an hearth. My heart is smitten, and withered like grass; so that I forget to eat my bread. By reason of the voice of my groaning my bones cleave to my skin. I am like a pelican of the wilderness: I am like an owl of the desert. I watch, and am as a sparrow alone upon the housetop. Mine enemies reproach me all the day; and they that are mad against me are sworn against me. For I have eaten ashes like bread, and mingled my drink with weeping. My days are like a shadow that declineth; and I am withered like grass."

Notice the connotations dealing with fire: days consumed like smoke, bones burned as an hearth, ashes like bread, and grass burnt by the sun. The feeling of desolation and loneliness is vivid in every line; he becomes like a pelican, not an eagle. He is forced to remain in the pit of burning despair: hot, scorched, smoky, and forsaken.

Verse 9 underlines the end-of-the-rope feeling. "I have eaten ashes like bread, and mingled my drink with weeping." You sit alone while your tears fall into your drink mocking you as they disappear into the glass. The ashes have become so abundant that they have intruded into your life as a common everyday staple. You feed on them so long that they become as familiar as your face. You go to your mental cupboard and there are many loaves waiting for you to consume. The bakery of despair never shuts down; it constantly produces more.

As you eat the bread you cry as Job cried, "And now my soul is poured out upon me; the days of affliction have taken hold upon me. My bones are pierced in me in the night season: and my sinews take no rest . . . I am become like dust and ashes" (Job 30:16-17,19).

Not only is your mind in torment, but desperation is seemingly resident in your whole body. You have eaten the ashes so long that you have become like them. There is a process. First the hurt, then the anger and grieving, finally the building of the shrine. A shrine is not built by one thought, but it is one thought placed upon another until it becomes big enough to bow down before. Without realizing it a large portion of your day is now delegated to paying homage to the thing that dominates you. It is not enough to have been hurt — now you suffer the torment of reliving it all. It becomes the thing you give the most attention to, and all the while it is slowly destroying you.

Shrines built out of ashes are just that: ashes without any substance. Ashes by themselves offer only empty promises, deceit, and hopelessness, with nothing to build upon in the future. Sifting through the ashes until you blend in with them, you become just one solitary figure searching for something to insure peace of mind, but it seems so hard to find.

The winds of adversity seem to blow even harder as the ashes cover you from head to foot. Where once there was clarity of thought now there is dimmed thinking and limited vision. All is changed; you feel like the charred log that the ashes originated from, blackened and now a powdery gray. The gray matches your spirit. It is not red with excitement, or yellow with warmth. It is just a dull, colorless, non-existent substance that reduces you to just a shell of your former self. Cheerless, dismal, and desolate is the state of mind that causes you to build a shrine that will destroy you eventually.

Where did all this hurt come from? There would be no pain if the serpent had never deceived Adam and Eve. Remember, your enemy, the devil, is trying to get you down. He has, as he did to Job, caused a temporary breakdown in your life. Your enemy watches you fall, and then when you stay down he goes away laughing because he succeeded in keeping you there. He did what he set out to do: to make you bitter, unforgiving, and disillusioned. He cannot be happy, so he does not want you to be happy. You can either build a shrine of bitterness, fear, unforgiveness, or hate, or you can rise and begin again. Before we talk about the resurrection out of the ash pile, let us examine the four shrines mentioned above.

4

THE SHRINE OF BITTERNESS

Bitterness is a painful, distressful, grievous feeling. It is piercingly cold to the soul and causes one to express grief or pain. Bitterness, unchecked, can develop into animosity, cruelty, or harshly reproachful, biting, caustic feelings, actions, or speech.

Shakespeare once said, "How bitter a thing it is to look into happiness through another man's eyes!"[1] The person who hurt you may appear to be happy and that can be galling to you because you want them to hurt like you are hurting.

Shakespeare also made reference to enemies by this statement, "Eating the bitter bread of banishment."[2] There is nothing much worse than rejection. To be shunned by someone or replaced by another is humiliating, hurtful, and tears at the soul. You cry, "What have I done? Why are there walls instead of love? How can they be so blind? Don't they see how they are hurting me? I've given them so much, and now they walk away like there was nothing there.

Where is the loyalty? Where is the friendship and love we once shared? How can they give their allegiance to someone else when it is hurtful to me?"

Sometimes life hands you sorrow, distress, and extreme difficulties. This happened to a beautiful dark-eyed Jewish girl name Hannah. Biblical history tells us that, "Her adversary also provoked her sore, for to make her fret . . . . therefore she wept, and did not eat . . . . And she was in **bitterness** of soul, and prayed unto the Lord, and wept sore" (1 Sam. 1:6-7,10).

Hannah was the favorite wife of Elkanah, a Levite of Ramathaim-zophim, who belonged to one of the most honorable families. Elkanah followed the common custom of polygamy in those days when "every man did that which was right in his own eyes." Elkanah's second wife, Peninnah, was a cruel and caustic woman. Her cruelty manifested itself on the day of the feast at Shiloh when she provoked Hannah to tears. Her husband asked, "What's wrong, Hannah?"

Hannah was so deeply hurt because of the constant friction and scurrilous tongue of Peninnah that she arose quickly from the table and went straight to the temple to pray. It was not easy for her to live with such a hateful woman year after year; it became a very heavy burden. When the load became unbearable Hannah carried her trial and yearning to God in prayer. Her bitterness of soul caused her to cry out to God. She did not keep it bottled inside of her, but drew peace from the Peacegiver.

Psalm 102:17 says, "He will regard the prayer of the destitute, and not despise their prayer."

The only way you can get rid of bitterness is to pray to the Lord. God will help you release those deep hurts. Paul describes how it is without God in Romans 3:10-18.

Bitterness in the soul expresses itself sooner or later by the tongue. Paul categorizes bitterness with the tongue in Ephesians 4:31. "Let all bitterness, and wrath, and anger, and clamour, and evil speaking, be put away from you, with all malice."

An old Latin proverb says, "He who goes to bed angry has the devil for a bedfellow." Never take your enemies to bed with you. You never know when the fatal blow is going to come.

Anger and bitterness is like a volcano within your breast erupting from time to time from out of the mouth, causing a clamorous wind to blow on the listener. The wind and fire caused from the volcano will affect everyone it touches.

The story is told about a man who was a heavy smoker, and became annoyed when his friends helped themselves liberally to his expensive Havana cigars. He decided to play a trick on them. He had a tobacconist construct a lot of cigars made entirely of cabbage leaves and brown paper wrapping. He left these on his desk and a day later, departed for a short trip. When he returned, his Havanas started disappearing again.

"But what did you do with those new cigars I ordered," he asked his secretary?

"Oh, those," said his secretary, "I took it for granted that those were something special. So I put that box in your suitcase."

"My God!" exclaimed the man. "You mean to say that I smoked every one of those things myself?"

It always seems to work that way. He was the only one who suffered any loss in his scheme when he tried to shut out others from what he considered to be his own private world. Sometimes people enter our world and take things that are dear to us. We then scheme and plan how to hurt them and the plan backfires in our face, because we are the ones filled with bitterness and it poisons us. A spirit of bitterness is worse than the hurt because it becomes rooted in us and spreads like a cancerous tree throughout our whole system.

There once was a high fence built on a prominent boulevard in Chicago. A woman placed it there who imagined her neighbor was peering into her windows. It did cut off the neighbor's view, but it shut the sunshine out of her own yard, ruined the lawn, and cast a shadow upon the house. Resentment and bitterness cast the heaviest shadow over the heart that harbors them, and shuts out life's sunshine.

Hebrews 12:14-15 tells us to "Follow peace with all men, and holiness, without which no man shall see the Lord: Looking diligently lest any man fail of the grace of God; lest any root of bitterness springing up trouble you, and thereby many be defiled." Everyone who comes within the radius of your presence or influence will feel your spirit and has the chance to be defiled by the root of bitterness.

Sometimes small offenses take place and there is not forgiveness, just a brushing over them until finally, all those little seeds get together and form a tough root. Big crushing experiences of human relationships do not happen overnight. Many small happenings and hurts fuse them together. If you have been burnt because of many offenses that piled up and then a big blowup took place, do not feel like all is lost. Forgive, get up, and begin again a much wiser person.

The following story tells how important it is to take care of small things in order to keep the blessing of the Lord in your life. One night when Mr. Moody, founder of Moody Bible Institute, was leading the singing and Mr. Sankey was playing the organ, Moody looked over to Sankey and said, "Excuse me; I see a friend coming into the meeting. I offended him today downtown, and I want him to forgive me."

Mr. Moody walked down from the platform toward the other man. The other man got up from his seat and walked out into the aisle and met Mr. Moody about halfway, and said, "Mr. Moody, I forgive you heartily."

Moody went back to the platform, and an eyewitness said, "I never saw such a meeting; it was wonderful." That is why God so richly used Mr. Moody. He kept a conscience that was void of offense toward God.

People can have a falling out over unimportant things until it consumes their whole life causing misery and hate. There were two neighbors who had a dispute over the boundary line between their farms. Feelings became so intense that each built his own fence about four feet apart. This just added extra expense for a four-foot strip of land that was useless. Everyone around them called it, "The Devil's Lane."

The two families would not speak to each other over four feet of land. For years they lived miserable lives, seething with resentment. They were under the control of their real enemy, the devil. He manufactures hate, bitterness, and unhappiness.

Hate and bitterness go hand in hand. You cannot have one without the other. Booker T. Washington once made a wise statement. He said, "I am determined to permit no man to narrow or degrade my soul by making me hate him."[3]

March 4, 1865, ushered in one of the greatest speeches ever made on the inauguration platform. The crowd grew silent as Abraham Lincoln stepped forward to make his address. He talked straight from his heart and the audience sensed the emotion and importance of the hour. He began:

On the occasion corresponding to this four years ago, all thoughts were anxiously directed to an impending civil war . . . . All knew that slavery was, somehow, the cause of the war . . . . Neither party expected for the war the magnitude or the duration which it has already attained . . . . Each looked for an easier triumph . . . . Both read the same Bible, and pray to the same God; and each invokes His aid against the other . . . . It may seem strange that any men should dare to ask a just God's assistance in wringing their bread from the sweat of other men's faces; but let us judge not, that we be not judged.[4]

There was no political phraseology, he was asking for peace and tolerance, for understanding and an end to bitterness and strife. He closed with this passage:

With malice toward none; with charity for all; with firmness in the right, as God gives us to see the right, let us strive on to finish the work we are in; to bind up the nation's wounds; to care for him who shall have borne the battle, and for his widow and his orphan — to do all which may achieve and cherish a just and lasting peace among ourselves and with all nations.[4]

Bitterness and hate caused the war that tore the country apart, separated brothers, and destroyed homes, property, and families. Bitterness never wins. It is a losing game. Everyone who is touched by it feels the smirch of filth and degradation. It is a shrine that should be avoided as one would avoid a rattlesnake. You have to guard against it, because if you live long enough you will have an excuse to become bitter.

You have to take charge of the situation. You either ride life or it rides you. You have to take the reins in your hand and call out the directions. If you do not, it will direct you. You can have faith to direct if you are founded on the Rock, Christ Jesus.

George W. Boschke was the famous engineer who built the gigantic sea wall to protect Galveston, Texas, from the horrible floods which had brought disaster to the city. He built his sea wall with a sure confidence of a thoroughgoing engineer and master workman. From Galveston he went to Oregon to build railroads in an undeveloped section of the state. Boschke was in a camp forty miles away from the nearest railroad when an exhausted messenger rode in and handed a telegram to his assistant. The message said that the Galveston sea wall had been washed away by a second furious hurricane. The assistant was in consternation and dreaded to hand the telegram to his chief. Boschke read the telegram, smiled, handed it back and said, "The telegram is a black lie. I built that wall to stand."

He turned away and went about his work. It turned out that the message was based on a false report. True, there had been a hurricane as severe as that which had flooded the city before, but Boschke's sea wall had not been moved. It stood firm. "I built that wall to stand," said Boschke and went smiling about his work amid rumors of disaster.[5]

The only rock to build upon is the rock the wise man built on. The storms came to the wise man and the foolish man alike, but the house of the wise man stood firm. Storms will come to you, contrary winds will blow, and you will be "burnt" by other people, but stand strong on the rock and let it polish you to becoming more like Christ.

The Shrine of Bitterness is built out of ashes and will someday fade into the wind of time scattering poisonous memories. Instead of building with the ashes of bitterness, build on the strong rock of Christ and know power and freedom.

5

THE SHRINE OF UNFORGIVENESS

Just before Leonardo da Vinci started to work on his great painting, *The Last Supper*, he had a violent quarrel with a fellow painter. He was so angry and bitter that he determined to paint the face of his enemy, the other artist, into the face of Judas. He wanted each succeeding generation to look with scorn upon his friend. The face of Judas was one of the first he finished, and everyone could easily recognize it as the face of the painter with whom he had quarreled.

When he came to paint the face of Christ, he could make no progress. Something seemed to be holding him back and frustrating his best efforts. At length he came to the conclusion that the thing which was confusing and frustrating him was that he had painted his enemy into the face of Judas. So he painted out the face of Judas and began again to work on the face of Jesus. So successful were his efforts that the picture has been acclaimed as one of the greatest paintings ever.

You cannot at the same time be painting the feature of Christ into your own life, and painting another face with the colors of enmity and hatred. Unforgiveness will hinder our relationship with God and cause our prayers not to be answered. In Mark we read, "What things soever ye desire when ye pray, believe that ye receive them, and ye shall have them. And when ye stand praying, forgive ..." (Mark 11:24-25).

Forgiveness is the key which unlocks the door of hatred and resentments. It breaks the chains of hardcore bitterness. We are told to love one another, but sometimes it seems impossible to do so. "Seeing ye have purified your souls in obeying the truth through the Spirit unto **unfeigned** love of the brethren, see that ye **love** one another with a pure heart fervently" (1 Pet. 1:22).

Unfeigned means genuine love; not counterfeit or hypocritical. You may say, "I cannot forgive and love in that measure." You are right! You cannot by yourself, but God can love through you. In Corrie Ten Boom's book, *Corrie Ten Boom, Her Life — Her Faith,* she tells of her struggle with hatred and how the Holy Spirit helped her to love. This is the story of her reaction to a guard who was evil to her and her family in the Ravensbruck Prison during World War II.

Corrie encountered one of her biggest challenges in Berlin. Many meetings were planned for her, and at the close of each talk she would counsel with people one at a time. One evening she was tired and very impatient. A man stood in the corner of the inquiry room and waited until everyone had left. When Corrie looked at him, she thought, *I wouldn't like to meet him in a dark street when I was alone.* Finally she turned to him, anxious to end her counseling and go home.

"How can I help you?" she asked.

He looked down and didn't answer. Corrie became sharper in her tone. "Listen, sir, if you won't speak up, I don't know how to help you."

When she saw the despair in his face, she regretted her attitude and started to silently pray for wisdom during the rest of the conversation.

When he spoke, Corrie knew why he was so hesitant. Her body stiffened as he said. "I am one of the guards of Ravensbruck. I was there at the time that you were one of the prisoners. At Christmas time I accepted Jesus Christ as my Saviour. I repented of my sins, but then I asked, 'God, give me the opportunity to ask one of my victims forgiveness.' That's why I'm here. Will you forgive me?"

Corrie said she felt a warmth flow through her arm that forced the stiff hatred from her heart. She reached out her hand to grasp his, it was as if God's love flowed through her. "I forgive you for everything," she said, and then opened her Bible. She read 1 John 1:7,9: "In these verses it is written that your sins are forgiven. Isn't it a joy that we may believe it?"

The former concentration camp guard covered his face and sobbed, "But I can't forget my sins."

Corrie's simple but biblically sound explanation was, "Jesus will blot out your sins like a cloud. A cloud does not return. He will put your sins away as far as the east is from the west. If you repent, He casts them into the depths of the sea, forgiven and forgotten. Then He puts out a sign, NO FISHING ALLOWED."

Without the experience of forgiving her enemies, Corrie's messages would have been hollow. Forgiveness, however, was not an emotion that happened once and then continued without interruption.

Another prison guard, Carl, had been sentenced to sixteen years imprisonment in the jail at Vught, the very place where he had practiced his cruelties. Corrie was shown a letter from Carl while she was in Germany, in which he said that he had accepted Jesus as his Saviour. After reading this, Corrie decided to request an amnesty for him from Queen Juliana. Before she wrote to her queen, however, she decided to go to Vught to see Carl.

She walked into the courtyard where she and Betsie had stood, trembling with the memory of the Dutchmen who were shot before their eyes. When she met Carl, he said to her, "How happy I am that my sins have been taken away."

For a moment Corrie had the same doubts so many of us have felt. Is forgiveness that simple? Here was a man who was part of the barbarism that caused many people to die. Was he really no longer guilty?

Corrie wrote: "It is an immutable law of

God that man finds peace only when he is continually ready to forgive. Suddenly I see what I am doing. Carl's sins have been cast by Jesus into the depths of the sea. They are forgiven and forgotten—and I am trying to fish them up again."

Corrie learned a lesson in Carl's cell. When Jesus requires that we love our enemies, He gives us the love He demands from us. We are channels of His love, not reservoirs. A reservoir can spring a leak, and all the love could be drained away. A channel provides the method for a continuous flow from the oceans of God's love.[1]

You might say, "Well, maybe I could forgive them if they have been forgiven by God, but if they continue to burn and hurt me, that is a different story." You can either continue to harbor unforgiveness, burn with resentment inside, and develop disease and bitterness, or you can do it God's way which is liberating.

John Huss, the courageous pastor of Prague, was arrested, condemned, and sentenced to be burned by a church council in 1415. When Huss heard his sentence pronounced, he fell to his knees and prayed, "Lord Jesus, forgive my enemies." Then when he was chained to the stake, he prayed, "In Thee, O Lord, do I put my trust; let me never be ashamed."

Notice the very ones he associated with were the ones who orchestrated his death, simply because they did not understand his new revelation. Even though they were able to kill his flesh, they could not embitter him or kill his spirit. He was the real winner.

The Sermon on the Mount is filled with many instructions for us to follow. One of them is how to treat people who hurt us. He said, "Ye have heard that it hath been said, Thou shalt love thy neighbour, and hate thine enemy. But I say unto you, Love your enemies, bless them that curse you, do good to them that hate you, and pray for them which despitefully use you, and persecute you; That ye may be the children of your Father which is in heaven: for he maketh his sun to rise on the evil and on the good, and sendeth rain on the just and on the unjust. For if ye love them which love you, what reward have ye? do not even the publicans the same? And if ye salute your brethren only, what do ye more than others? do not even the publicans so? Be ye therefore perfect, even as your Father which is in heaven is perfect" (Matt. 5:43-48).

One eyewitness related that he saw Christians in Communist prisons with fifty pounds of chains on their feet, tortured with red-hot iron pokers, in whose throats spoonfuls of salt had been forced, being kept afterward without water, starving, whipped, suffering from cold, and praying with fervor for the Communists. Later some of the Communists were put in the same prison with the Christians. There the Christians gave away their last slice of bread and the medicine which could save their lives to a sick Communist torturer who was now a fellow prisoner. **That is forgiveness!**

If we indulge in hate and unforgiveness, we are giving our enemy power over us. Blood pressure, health, sleep, skin, and happiness are all affected by our emotions. The hate and unforgiveness turns inward and life becomes one swirling turmoil of unrest, for an angry unforgiving person is full of poison.

In 1946, Czeslaw Godlewski was a member of a young gang that roamed and sacked the German countryside. On an isolated farm they gunned down ten members of the Wilhelm Hamelmann family. Nine of the victims died, but Hamelmann himself survived his four bullet wounds.

When Godlewski completed a twenty-year prison term for his crimes the state would not release him because he had nowhere to go. When Hamelmann learned of the situation, he asked the authorities to release Godlewski to his custody. He wrote in his request, "Christ died for my sins and forgave me. Should I not then forgive this man?"

Godlewski obeyed Romans 12:20. "Therefore if thine enemy hunger, feed him; if he thirst, give him drink: for in so doing thou shalt heap coals of fire on his head." Burn them with kindness, and the fire that was meant to destroy will backfire.

When the disciple Peter asked Jesus how often he had to forgive someone who had done him wrong, Jesus answered him with words that must have shocked Peter: seventy times seven. Then Jesus explained what He meant as He so often did. He told the story of a king which took account of his servants. He found one which owed him ten thousand talents. He told the servant that he had to pay him the money he owed, but the servant did not have the money to pay. The king then commanded him to be sold, and his wife, and children, and all that he had so he could pay his debt.

The servant fell down and worshipped him saying, "Lord, have patience with me, and I will pay thee all. Then the lord of that servant was moved with compassion, and loosed him, and forgave him the debt." Then the same servant went out and found one of his fellow servants which owed him an hundred pence. He laid hands on him and took him by the throat and demanded that he pay him right then. The fellow servant fell down and begged for mercy, but the other servant would not listen to his pleas. Instead he had him thrown into a debtor's prison.

When the king heard about what had happened out in the street, he called his servant in and said to him, "O thou wicked servant, I forgave thee all that debt, because thou desiredst me: Shouldest not thou also have had compassion on thy fellow servant, even as I had pity on thee? And his lord was wroth, and delivered him to the tormentors, till he should pay all that was due unto him." Jesus ended the discussion with these words, "So likewise shall my heavenly Father do also unto you, if ye from your hearts forgive not every one his brother their trespasses" (Matt. 18:21-35).

Do you have trouble forgiving others? Is it easier to hold grudges? Try doing this for twenty-one days. Every night when you go to bed, pray and ask God to do a work inside your heart. Then read these words over and let them be in your sub-conscious mind as you drift off to sleep and when you arise in the morning:

> Today is a new day. In the past I have accepted bitterness and unforgiveness, but as of now I reject it. My mind is instead being filled with God's wisdom. I have lived as a chicken scratching in the barnyard, but now I will soar with the eagles, for I have learned to wait and meditate on the Lord. I will think on the Lord and His principles, for they are life and power.

> This day I choose to have love in my heart, for love is the answer to all problems. God is love and if I have God He will give me the love and forgiveness that I need. I will

look for reasons to do good to all people, forgetting what getting even means. I will walk with love in my heart and beam love to all that I meet. I was made to soar and live in victory through Christ. I will accept what He has offered to me, as a child would accept something from a loving father.

In Christ I have power to forgive, live, and rise again from the ash heap of bitterness and hate. If God be for me, who can be against me? I will win because I am on the winning side. This day is the first day of the rest of my life, so I will live it well, walking as a child of the King should walk.

6

THE SHRINE OF FEAR

The Shrine of Fear that is erected out of the ashes is a very painful emotion marked by alarm. It characterizes dread, panic, terror, and anticipation of danger or continual hurt. This shrine takes up residence in the mind and crowds out hope and faith imprisoning the one who fears.

In 1972, two hunters on the island of Guam discovered a man hiding in the jungle whose story shocked the world. In 1944 a Japanese soldier fled to Guam when the tides of war began to change. Fearing for his life, he stayed hidden, coming out only at night. For twenty-eight years he lived on snails, shrimp, rats, frogs, nuts, and mangoes. When his clothes wore out he made burlap-like clothes from tree bark.

After being found by the two men, he said he knew the war was over because of the leaflets he found scattered throughout the jungle, but he was afraid that if he came out of his hiding place he would be killed. The hunters told him he was free, that his fears were groundless, and that he could go home.

How like the soldier so many are, living in self-imposed prisons, afraid to venture forth, always hiding, just existing instead of truly living. Because of a previous frightening experience they just dig in somewhere and never surface again.

Fear not only affects you; it affects others as well. A Los Angeles newspaper reported a story about a woman who was driving down the road when she looked up and saw a group of men running out of a bank with machine guns. She lost control of her car, struck five pedestrians, and slammed into two other cars, which hit two more people.

The tragedy of it all was the fact that her fears were groundless. The machine-gun-toting hold-up men were part of a Hollywood bank hold-up scene. The guns were not loaded and the bank was not even real. A bank-like front had been set up in front of a store.

Your cause for fear may be real, but nothing is worth losing control over your life as the woman did with her car. Things will happen which will hurt you and beckon fear to come and settle in your mind and consciousness. Keep steady; do not panic. You can win over fear; if you do not, fear will kill you.

In a sermon entitled, "Fear," Rev. Clarence Macartney gives an illustration that proves this. A peasant man driving into an European city was stopped by an elderly woman asking for a ride. As they drove along, she told him she had cholera. When he became alarmed, she assured him that only ten people in the city would die from it. Then she gave him a dagger telling him that he could kill her with it if she was proven wrong.

When they entered the city it was discovered that

more than a hundred had died. When the angry, fearful peasant drew the dagger to kill, she lifted her head and protested, "Wait, I killed only ten! Fear killed the rest!"

The legendary "Blood and Guts" General George Patton, who served his country in World War II and led his men to victory many times, often made the statement to his men: "Fear kills more people than death."

There will always be the potential of fear in every situation, but it is intensified when there has been a burning or hurtful experience. You will never outgrow fear, but you can conquer fears. You do not have to bow down before its tyrannical rule. It is a cruel taskmaster.

An Indian fable is told that illustrates the principle that you will always have something to fear if you choose to worship at the Shrine of Fear. One day there was a mouse who was in great distress, filled with fear because of a cat. So the village witch doctor turned the mouse into a cat because he felt sorry for the poor little mouse. The only trouble was that when he became a cat he was fearful of the dog. So he turned him into a dog. The dog became afraid of a tiger so the magician turned him into a tiger and the tiger started fearing the hunter. Finally the magician said, "Be a mouse again, you have only the heart of a mouse and I cannot help you."

It is not enough to change locations, clothes, jobs, or hairstyles. There must be change of heart. One must realize that it is not what you have lost that is important, it is what you have left that counts. The fear of losing again or being burnt again will keep your eyes on yesterday, but yesterday is only ashes.

The story of Harold Russell who rose from the ash

heap of life to success was so inspirational that it was made into a motion picture called *The Best Years of Our Life*. Millions viewed it and were challenged to never give up even when it looked like all was lost.

While Harold was serving in World War II, one day he woke up in a hospital bed with the greatest shock of his life: both of his hands were gone. He was filled with dread and terror when he thought of life with no hands. He really did not care whether he lived or died, until one day Charlie McGonegal, who had lost both his hands in World War I came to visit him.

Charlie told him that in order to make it he must first conquer himself and get rid of his bitterness and fear. He said something that struck a chord in Russell's mind. "You are not crippled; you are merely handicapped." The more he thought about it the more curious he became. He went to the library and looked up the two words. Crippled means "disabled, incapable of proper or effective action." Handicapped means "any disadvantage or hindrance making success or undertaking more difficult."

This jarred his thinking. As he had many hours to recuperate, he decided to stop thinking on what he had lost and concentrate on what he had left. As a result of the handicap and his new way of thinking, he found a new way of life. He decided to help others with their fears and regain hope. He became an inspiration to many as an author, radio personality, and speaker.

In one of his books he wrote these words: "I don't think I'd ever willingly lose my hands, if I had it to do all over again. But having lost them, I feel perhaps I have gained many fine things I might never have had with them. The important thing is that this seeming disaster has brought me a priceless wealth of the spirit that I am sure I could not have possessed otherwise. I have enjoyed a life that has had meaning and depth it never had before. It is not what you have lost, but what you have left that counts. Too many of us squander precious energy, time, and courage dreaming of things that were and never can be again, instead of dedicating ourselves to realities and the heavy tasks of today.

"People marvel at the things I can do with my hooks. But the thing I never cease to marvel at is that I was able to meet the challenge of utter disaster and master it . . . that the human soul, beaten down, overwhelmed, faced by complete failure and ruin, can still rise up against unbearable odds and triumph."[1]

Helen Keller, who was blind, said, "I thank God for my handicaps, for through them I have found myself, my work, and my God."

You do not always choose what happens to you, but if something painful does happen to you, you can choose as Harold Russell and Helen Keller did. Choose whether you will be mentally and emotionally crippled — incapable of effective action; or handicapped — a disadvantage that makes success more difficult. You can overcome your fears, but you have to stop bowing down to the Shrine of Fear and letting it dominate your thinking.

Life will have its pain and pockets of fear. One cannot walk on mountain peaks. There will be rivers to cross, valleys to walk through, treacherous routes and obstacles along the way. What they do to you determines how much fight you have in you. You can become stronger because of life's experiences, but you must *will* it to be.

It was Seneca, the writer of old, who said, "Just as so many rivers, so many showers of rain from above, so many medicinal springs do not alter the taste of the sea, so the pressure of adversity does not affect the mind of the brave man. For it maintains its balance, and over all that happens it throws its own complexion, because it is more powerful than external circumstances."[2]

God can give you inner peace and take away your fear so you *can* stand strong in the time of fearful circumstances. In 2 Timothy 1:7, Paul gives hope. "For God hath not given us a spirit of fear; but of power, and of love, and of a sound mind." Fear is a spirit, but that spirit can be dominated by God's power. You do not have to get rid of fear by yourself. Your will is not always strong enough, but with God all things are possible. He makes up the difference.

Do not try to face your difficulties and fears alone. It was Francis Bacon who said, "I can remember the days when people talked about the conflict between science and religion. But no more. The newest of all sciences — psychiatry — is teaching what Jesus taught. Why? Because psychiatrists realize that prayer and a strong religious faith will banish the worries, the anxieties, the strains, and *fears* that cause more than half of all our ills. They know, as one of their leaders, Dr. A.A. Brill, said: 'Anyone who is truly religious does not develop a neurosis.' "[3]

Nearing the end of his life Henry Ford was asked if he ever worried or feared. He replied, "No, I believe God is managing affairs and that He doesn't need any advice from me. With God in charge, I believe that everything will work out for the best in the end. So what is there to worry about?"

He could say that in his older years. He had learned to conquer his fears and worries by trusting in God. The brave man is not he who feels no fear, but he who subdues his fear. One who will go forward in the face of danger knowing that God is with him.

The story is often told of David facing Goliath on the battlefield during the war between the Philistines and the Israelites. All the Israelite soldiers were shaking in their boots, afraid to face Goliath. When David walked into camp that day, little did he know what he was going to face. His confidence in God took precedence over his fear. He faced the very thing that everyone else was afraid of, because he chose not to stand in his own might, but in the might of the Lord.

His faith canceled his fear. When he started down the mountain toward the bellowing nine-foot Goliath, his mind was not on the height nor the threats coming from the giant's mouth. He was filled with excitement because he knew in whom he believed. When Goliath challenged David and his God, David knew that the battle was already won. The battle ceased to be his; it now was between God and Goliath.

That little stone that was flung from that slingshot probably was carried by either the Spirit of the Lord or an angel, a messenger from God. Whichever way it happened, David proved that trust in God took away fear. He did not say, "I am coming to you in my power," but he said, "I come to you in the name of the Lord."

This day determine in your heart that you will venture forth upon an excursion of faith. This trial will not always be. You do not have to worship at this shrine. It will not set you free; it will imprison you. "It is cynicism and fear that freeze life; it is faith that thaws it out, releases it, sets it free" (Harry Emerson Fosdick).[4]

Freedom from fear can be yours; you must learn to rule your fears through God so they will not rule you. What is the motivating or ruling factor in your life — fear or faith? Whatever motivates you will influence your performance.

There is an old fable about a dog that boasted of his ability as a runner. One day he chased a rabbit and failed to catch it. The other dogs ridiculed him on account of his previous boasting. His reply was, "You must remember that the rabbit was running for his life, while I was only running for my dinner." It does make a difference if we are doing the chasing or we are being chased.

This day determine to be motivated or ruled by faith. Get out of the ash pile and stop bowing down to the Shrine of Fear by consciously making an effort to do so, just as Harold Russell, Helen Keller, and David did. Let us chase fear out of our life instead of fear dogging our footsteps. Say, as David said, "Fear, I come to you in the name of the Lord, and tell you to get out of my mind." Stand firm upon the powerful Word of God and implant it deeply in your mind and you are on your way to victory.

7

THE SHRINE OF HOPELESSNESS

The voice on the other end of the phone sobbed hopelessly with a ragged edge to the words. Desperately from way down she spoke, "I can't go on living this way. Nothing works! It's getting worse by the day! I just can't see any good in any of this." She continued on almost hysterically, "Life is a nightmare! I can't stand it any longer. Please, help me. There's nowhere to turn, just no way out; it's hopeless." Then the tears and brokenness came over the line like a bursting dam of water. My tears joined hers and fervently I prayed as the sobbing grew less and less.

She had erected the Shrine of Hopelessness; hope was banished and she lived in the land where all was blackness. Not a drop of sunshine could be found anywhere. She had tried everything and everything had failed. Where could she go, what could she do? Was there life after the death of her marriage? Could she ever smile again?

Hopelessness is despair, despondency, and destitution. Job experienced this. He said, "Wearisome nights are appointed to me. When I lie down, I say, When shall I arise, and the night be gone? and I am full of tossings to and fro unto the dawning of the day. My flesh is clothed with worms and clods of dust; my skin is broken, and become loathsome. My days are swifter than a weaver's shuttle, and are spent without hope" (Job 7:3-6).

There is a sad story told of one of the tragedies of World War II. An aircraft carrier was out in the North Atlantic. As it was engaged in war, its six pilots took off the carrier to scout out some enemy submarines. While these pilots were gone, the captain of the ship issued an alarm. The button was pushed, and every light on the ship was extinguished.

As the pilots started to come back toward the mother ship, they could not find her, so radioed the ship, "Give us light, we're coming home."

The radio operator on the ship radioed back: "Order — blackout. I can't give you light."

Another pilot picked up his radio and desperately said, "Just give us some light, and we'll make it."

The radio operator said, "No light — blackout."

The third pilot picked up his radio and asked for the same thing, and received the same answer as the other pilots. The operator could do no more. He reached over, turned the switch, and broke radio contact. Six aviators in the prime of life went down in the cold north Atlantic Ocean.

That was hopelessness personified. This story portrays what happens when someone erects the Shrine of Hopelessness, for if you have no hope, you die. You cannot live very long without hope. Although this story is sad and shows what hopelessness really is like, it does not paint the true picture of life.

These men were dealing with a system, but you are dealing with God. That is the difference. The devil would also like you to believe that God's communication system is broken down or turned off and that He will not or is unable to help you.

The secret of dealing with hopelessness is found in Psalm 43:5, "Why art thou cast down, O my soul? and why art thou disquieted within me? hope in God: for I shall yet praise him, who is the health of my countenance, and my God." Powerful words: HOPE IN GOD.

An artist once painted a very desolate picture of a wintry scene with a darkened house sitting on the side of a rocky hill. The wind was whistling, the trees were bowing down; the colors he used were all gray, black, and brown. To look at it gave one a chill ... until ... the artist took a yellow tube of paint and placed it on his palette. Dipping his brush into the bright yellow, he dabbed it in all the windows of the little house; and light shone out to all around. One stroke of light and hopelessness turned to hope.

Jesus said, "I am the light of the world: he that followeth me shall not walk in darkness, but shall have the light of life" (John 8:12). It does not matter how dark your world is, with Jesus helping you, light comes into the picture. There is hope in Him. Things may not get better over night, but they will get better! Instead of giving up and bowing down before the Shrine of Hopelessness, say with the apostle Paul, "Lord Jesus Christ, which is our hope" (1 Tim. 1:1).

Psalm 71:13-14 gives a prayer concerning a circumstance that is hurtful and then shows the right attitude one should have when going through such a time. "Let them be confounded and consumed that are adversaries to my soul; let them be covered with reproach and dishonour that seek my hurt. But I will hope continually, and will yet praise thee more and more."

Again the promise is given in Psalm 72:12, "For he shall deliver the needy when he crieth, the poor also, and him that hath no helper." If you are alone, despondent, without hope, and no one to help you, God has promised to deliver you from the excruciating circumstance you are going through. So get up and live again. Hope in God, for He is your helper.

One unknown writer wrote, "Hope is like the sun, which, as we journey toward it, casts the shadow of our burden behind us."

Instead of focusing on the burden, focus on the light. Light dispels gloom. The following poem says it well:

> Be hopeful, friend, when clouds are dark and
>   days are gloomy, dreary,
> Be hopeful even when the heart is sick and
>   sad and weary.
> Be hopeful when it seems your plans are all
>   opposed and thwarted;
> Do not upon life's battlefield despondent and
>   fainthearted.
> And, friends, be hopeful of yourself.
> Do bygone follies haunt you?
> Forget them and begin afresh.
> And let no hindrance daunt you.
> Though unimportant your career may seem
>   as you begin it,
> Press on, for victory's ahead. Be hopeful,
>   friend, and win it.
>
> — Strickland Gillilan[1]

It has been said that it is always darkest before the dawn, and that there never was a night without a day, nor an evening without a morning. David said, "Weeping may endure for a night, but joy cometh in the morning" (Ps. 30:5). It may not be there with you right now, but it is on its way!

When we were little children growing up, we had to work before we played. Because there were six children there were a lot of things to do, so Mother assigned each child chores. I still remember sweating over the ironing board, washing clothes in the wringer washing machine, helping take the feathers off of the chickens, then singeing them over the flame. It seemed like there was so much to do, but something always gave us hope.

About mid-afternoon we could hear the ice-cream truck coming down the road playing circus music. That was our signal for a break. We ran out in the front yard with our nickels and dimes to wait for the truck which we knew was coming, but could not see. Sure enough, finally he got to our house and we had a time trying to decide which flavor we wanted.

This is the way joy is. You may not see it or feel it sometimes when the pain is unbearably intense, but you hear the music of God's Word playing in your mind, and you know it is coming. Get up and live again. Joy is coming. Hope in God!

It is time to do what Paul did. He said, "Brethren, I count not myself to have apprehended: but this one thing I do, forgetting those things which are behind, and reaching forth unto those things which are before, I press toward the mark for the prize of the high calling of God in Christ Jesus" (Phil. 3:13-14). Put yesterday behind you and reach up even when the enemy is shooting at you from every direction.

I have read the following story many times to my children when they were younger. It is taken from the Childcraft Series, Volume 12, *Pioneers and Patriots*. It describes exactly what you must do when everything is against you. You must keep going forward.

"All right, men," said the American general, "here is our plan of attack."

The soldiers stood silently, listening to their general's orders.

"Just ahead of us is Stony Point," the general said.

The men could see the large cliff that loomed up in the darkness. At the top of the cliff was the British fort, Stony Point.

"We are to attack Stony Point," the general went on. "The cliff is surrounded by water, but when the tide is low, which should be about midnight, we can wade across. We must have absolute silence, or our plan will fail.

"Our only chance is to surprise the British. We will advance in three columns. One column will climb the center of the cliff, the other two columns will climb on the right and left sides. When the center column gets near the top of the cliff, they will begin firing. My plan is to make the British think that the center column is our main army. In the meantime, the left and right columns will continue up the cliff and attack the fort from both sides. I know you will all fight like men determined to be free."

When the general finished talking, the troops were divided into three columns. It was close to midnight. The general gave the signal. The columns moved toward the cliff. The water around the cliff was still fairly deep and the men had to wade through water up to their waists. They held their muskets high above their heads and moved as quietly as possible. When they reached the cliff, they began the slow, steep climb toward the fort.

The general was with the left column. The tangle of branches up the side of the cliff was so thick that men had to chop through with axes. The sound of chopping was a great danger. If the British heard it, they would be able to stop the attack. Up, up they went. It was almost like scaling a wall, the cliff was so steep. But there was no sound from the fort.

Sleep sound and deep, British soldiers, thought the general. A wave of excitement swept over him, as often happened when he was in great danger. He remembered that one of his friends had said it would be impossible to capture Stony Point. *We can and we shall*, thought the general, as his column continued slowly up the cliff. And still the British were unaware of the coming attack.

In the quiet of the night the sound of chopping seemed loud. This time it reached the British. Gunfire came from the fort. *We have been discovered too soon*, the general thought. But then he saw that only the center column returned the fire. He hoped that the British did not yet know that columns were advancing from left and right. *We still have a chance*, he thought.

By now the Americans had nearly reached the fort. There was bound to be hard fighting, but the attack seemed to be going according to plan. From the sound of the guns, it seemed that the British had been tricked into thinking that the center column was the whole attacking army.

The general was pushing his way through the last tangle of branches, when a shot split the air. He felt something like a hard slap on the side of his head. Then there was nothing but blackness. He came to, lying just outside the branches with two of his men bending over him.

"He's wounded badly, but he's not dead," he heard a voice say. Then his mind cleared, and he knew where he was and why he was there.

"We'll take him back down the hill," said another voice.

"No!" the general snapped. Making a great effort, he sat up. "You will not take me back. Take me forward. If I die today, it will be at the head of my men."

Two men had to help him up the cliff. The troops were advancing rapidly now. The British were firing at all three columns of men, but they had discovered the plan too late. The left and right columns had nearly reached the fort by the time they were spotted. The general was with the wave of men who swept into the fort from both sides. The British fought bravely, but soon the battle was over.

"The fort is ours," shouted the general

above the cheers of his men. Then weakness from his head wound overtook him. The general slumped to the ground again.[2]

The general in this story was General Anthony Wayne, who was nicknamed "Mad Anthony" because he was never afraid to take risks. His attack in 1779 on Stony Point, an important British fort on the Hudson River, was considered to be one of the most daring of the Revolutionary War.

You may be wounded, but it is forward all the way. You can make it, just keep going. Never give up! Have hope and in time things will get better. The victory is yours, but sometimes you have to fight head-on with the enemy to get it. The secret is persistence even when it looks like all is lost. This is what helped win World War II. Half the British destroyers were in the shipyards for repairs, the Royal Air Force had lost 40 percent of its bomber strength, her armies were without arms or equipment, and Britain was on the brink of famine when Winston Churchill made his fiery, defiant, and challenging speech. He said, "We shall defend our island whatever the cost may be; we shall fight on the beaches; we shall fight in the fields; we shall fight in the streets; and we shall fight in the hill. We shall never surrender and if this island were subjugated and starving, our empire on the seas would carry on the struggle until in God's good time the New World with all its power and might steps forth to the rescue and liberation of the old."

Churchill just never did give up, and neither should you. Life is not promised to be without its sorrows and disappointments, but we were promised a helper in the time of trouble. Phillips Brooks preached to his congregation years ago the following thought:

"Do not pray for easy lives; pray to be strong men. Do not pray for tasks equal to your powers; pray for power equal to your tasks."

8

A JEWEL IN THE RUBBLE OF DESPAIR

You can find good in all experiences if you look long enough or give it time to emerge. You must be willing to find it and not let an angry, bitter spirit obscure it. When you look at Joseph and see the extraordinary events that took place in his life, you would be prone to say, "I cannot see God in that. Why would all that be necessary? Why did God allow him to be hurt so much?"

It is distressing to be rejected by one's own brothers and family and threatened to be killed by them. This happened to Joseph when he was just a young man. Try to mentally put yourself in his place. After they tantalized him with death, the older brother took mercy on him. Instead of killing Joseph, they sold him to a band of travelers who took him away from his home into a strange land. Then when he got there, he was sold as a slave into a wealthy man's home and the wife lied about Joseph's character. Because of her lies he was thrown into a dungeon where he lived innocently for two years. It is nothing you would have chosen, but Joseph did not choose it either.

Joseph did not become bitter, but kept a good attitude through all the times he was **burned** by others. His attitude always kept sending him to the top. It was his attitude of hope and faith that caused his brothers to be jealous of him in the first place. Because he was a dreamer and saw things in the future they did not see, they wanted to get rid of him. His dream got him in trouble, but it also got him out of trouble. His dream was not a selfish dream, but included God. God had his eye on Joseph during the whole scenario of his life. He never was alone even when he appeared to be.

Joseph summed up the story of his whole life with these words, "But as for you, ye thought evil against me; but God meant it unto good, to bring to pass, as it is this day, to save much people alive" (Gen. 50:20). He did not build a shrine of bitterness or harbor an unforgiving spirit, but instead kept his eye on his dream and his integrity with God.

Joseph had every right to be bitter according to human thinking. You also will be able to justify bitterness, unforgiveness, and hate by looking at the motive and person who burnt you. It is possible that you will have a good human reason for worshipping at the Shrine of Unforgiveness. Man's way is always destructive, but God's way is the path of life.

In every sorrow, there is a lesson to be learned; for adversity teaches us if we allow ourselves to be taught. Something good can flow out of the darkest prison of life. Paul's sweetest epistles were from prison cells, John's Revelation was written in exile, and John

Bunyan's *Pilgrim's Progress* came from the Bedford jail.

What are you writing during your time of trouble and anguish of soul? You can either cry, "Unfair," and let self-pity be your soul mate, or you can build a new life from the ashes.

Wallace Johnson, builder of numerous Holiday Inn motels and convalescent hospitals, told how when he was forty years old, he worked in a sawmill. One morning the boss told him, "You're fired!"

Depressed and discouraged, he felt like the world had caved in on him. When he went home, he told his wife what had happened. She simply asked, "What are you going to do now?"

That set him to thinking. He said, "I'm going to mortgage our little home, and go into the building business."

His first venture was the construction of two small buildings. Within five years, he was a multimillionaire! He said, "Today, if I could locate the man who fired me, I would sincerely thank him for what he did. At the time it happened I didn't understand why I was fired. Later, I saw that it was God's unerring and wondrous plan to get me into the way of His choosing!"

You may say, "Well, did God order my divorce? Did he order my accident? Did he cause my pain?" Probably not, but neither did He order Job's trouble. He said it would rain on the just and the unjust (Matt 5:45). This is an explanation for some happenings. Life will not be perfect. Other things are brought on because of our lack of caring about certain details — a cause and effect system. If you stay out in the snow long enough without a hat or coat on you will probably get sick. Then again there could be a contest between God and Satan, as in the case of Job. Trouble comes to all sooner or later. It is not the trouble that matters the most, but what we do with the trouble.

Troubles, struggles, and disappointments can make you beautiful inside if you will let them. It is how you react to the pain that tells what vessel you will become. There is on the coast of Pescadero, California, the famed Pebble Beach. The waves dash and roar continuously and make their way among the stones on the beach. The waves toss and grind the stones together and hurl them against the rugged cliffs. Day and night, the wearing down of the stones continues. Tourists from all over the world gather the beautiful, round, polished stones for ornaments and keepsakes.

Near Pebble Beach is a towering cliff which breaks the force of the dashing waves. There in a quiet cove, sheltered by the cliff, is an abundance of stones. These are not wanted because they have escaped the turmoil and beating of the waves. They have no beauty, but are rough and angular.

The waves of sorrow and trouble polish and refine us, and allow us to show forth the power of the Saviour's comforting, healing words. Many great things are born in the brokenness of our lives. It is the desperate times that demand greatness. Handel, the great composer was burned by circumstances and those that took advantage of him.

The aging composer, bowed by misfortune, wandered the lonely streets of London nightly in hopeless despair. Only memories of his past glory, when the brilliant man was touted by the court society of London and Europe, were left to him and it now seemed his musical genius was gone forever. George

Frederick Handel, once the favorite of kings and queens, had been forced into bankruptcy and had become a pauper.

One bitterly cold morning during the winter of 1741, Handel returned to his lodgings to find a thick package on the table. It contained a text made up of Scripture verses from the librettist Charles Jennens. Dazed by cold and hunger, Handel listlessly leafed through the pages.

"Comfort ye, comfort ye, My people, saith your God . . . . Behold! A virgin shall conceive and bear a Son, and shall call His name Emmanuel, God with us . . . . The people that walked in darkness have seen a great light . . . . For unto us a Child is born, unto us a Son is given . . . and His name shall be called Wonderful, Counsellor, The Mighty God . . . . Then shall the eyes of the blind be opened, and the ears of the deaf unstopped . . . . He shall feed His flock like a shepherd: and He shall gather the lambs with His arm, and carry them in His bosom . . . ."

Excitedly, he read on. "He was despised and rejected of men; a man of sorrows and acquainted with grief . . . . He looked for some to have pity on Him, but there was no man; neither found He any to comfort Him . . . . But thou didst not leave His soul in hell . . . ."

He hurriedly read on. "I know that my Redeemer liveth, and that He shall stand at the latter day upon the earth . . . . King of kings, and Lord of lords, Hallelujah!"

The Words burned into his soul and struck a responsive chord within him. He rushed to the piano with pencil in hand and began to write the music to the immortal *Messiah*. For two weeks he labored incessantly.

Handel saw no one and refused food and sleep. At last he finished the great oratorio and a friend was admitted to his room. Tears were streaming down his face. "I did think I did see all Heaven before me, and the great God himself," he declared of the completion of the glorious "Hallelujah Chorus."

The composition was first heard in Dublin where it was an overwhelming triumph. Several weeks later it was again a tumultuous success in London. During this performance the king, carried away by the glory of the great "Hallelujah Chorus," rose to his feet and the audience followed his example! Today, audiences all over the world still rise and remain standing during this chorus.

In succeeding years George Frederick Handel became blind, ill, and poor. But the composer of the great masterpiece never again permitted his misfortunes to overcome his spirit. [1]

You do not choose sorrow, but when it comes let it refine you. Sorrow teaches, for often the tear is the lens through which we see the formerly insignificant enlarged into eternal importance. Sorrow chastens and refines. It detaches us from the external, and gives us opportunity to become connected with the essential and permanent.

Blackwood's Magazine several years ago reported

these words of a great vocal teacher about one of his pupils:

"She sings well, but she lacks something, and that something is everything. If I were single I would court her; I would marry her; I would maltreat her; I would break her heart, and in six months she would be the greatest singer in Europe." The alabaster box must be crushed before the exquisite odors of the precious ointment are released.

Till the heart aches, it never knows its most exquisite joys. Songs in the night are usually sweet memories of the day of pain that is past. Touches of beauty are given to us by the gracious Spirit in the darkness though we cannot see. When sorrow teaches the heart, it tames wildness, softens asperities and makes it great with kindness and sympathy. And so, sorrow is not always a penalty for sin but a preparation for growth.[2]

Today if you will take an old stick and stir around in the ashes you will find a jewel that is shining underneath the hurts of it all. You have no promise of tomorrow, yesterday is history, you have only today. You are in charge of today. What are you doing with it?

Jewels can often be obscured by false fronts, obscure purposes, or misunderstandings. The value of a diamond is hidden beneath the black crusty exterior. It must be mined and brought to the surface before it can be of use to any one. During times of extreme pain and suffering, things that were lying hidden are exposed and jewels are discovered.

A wise and powerful king used to assume the dress of a peasant and tour through his domain to see in reality how his subjects fared. Stopping at a wayside inn for food and rest, he found it full of travelers. As he spoke to the innkeeper, instantly a knight stepped forward, and in tones which brought every man to his feet, exclaimed, "The dress may be that of a peasant, but the voice is that of my lord, the king."

This is the day to look for the jewel in the rubble of despair and not be overtaken by the flood of hurt and anger that would try to consume you.

TODAY

The best thing you have in this world is today. Today is your savior; it is often crucified between two thieves, yesterday and tomorrow.

Today you can be happy, not yesterday nor tomorrow. There is no happiness except today's.

Most of our misery is left over from yesterday or borrowed from tomorrow. Keep today clean. Make up your mind to enjoy your food, your work, your play — today anyhow.

You can do anything if you will only go at it a day at a time.

If you're bereaved, betrayed, heartbroken, why, take a day off. One day will not matter. Today put away your festering thoughts. Today take some simple joys. Today be a little happy in the sunshine. You can do it. It's the burden of the coming days, weeks, and years that crushes us. The present is always tolerable.

Why let life depress you? You don't have to live your life, only a day of it. Come, let's finish our small task manfully. It's not long.

Don't let life mass against you. Attack it in detail and you can triumph.

The past is what we make of it. It is the temper of the present that qualifies it. It depends upon how you now consider it, whether it brings you despair or encouragement.

Don't let the past unman you, benumb you with remorse, or weaken you with self-contempt.

The poet says we rise by stepping on our dead selves. And as for the future, the best preparation for it is an unafraid today.

If you are to die tomorrow, the best way to be ready is to discharge faithfully today's duties, and to enjoy heartily today's simple pleasures.

Today is yours. God has given it to you. All your yesterdays He has taken back. All your tomorrows are still in His hands.

Today is yours. Just a little strip of light between two darknesses.

Today is yours. Use it so that at its close you can say:

"I have lived, and loved, today!"

— Dr. Frank Crane[3]

9

BEAUTY FOR ASHES

God promised that if you would come to Him, He would take the leftovers or ashes of your life and give you beauty instead. You do not have to do it all yourself, for victory comes when you work together with God. Instead of building shrines which will destroy you, build altars to Him and He will restore you to a new life of beauty.

You may feel like your life is ugly and insignificant without much future. Sometimes things that appear ugly are just waiting for the right climate to grow. "There is a species of century plant called the maguey. It grows for years with great, coarse leaves, as thick as your two hands, broad as three, and long as twenty. It puts out sharp thorns, and is as ugly a thing as grows, and it gets worse all the time. But suddenly it shoots up in a few days a great shaft tall and thick as a small telegraph pole, and decks its spreading head with thousands of flowers. The possibility of all that fragrant beauty was always in that detestable ugliness."[1]

The fragrant beauty of your life is hidden sometimes underneath calloused ritual. It is smothered by daily schedules and monotonous grind. Sometimes painful experiences cause the beauty to come forth. It just needs God to cause it to flourish and grow from the ugliness of devastation into loveliness. Isaiah gives hope to all mankind.

> The Spirit of the Lord God is upon me: because the Lord hath anointed me to preach good tidings unto the meek; he hath sent me to bind up the brokenhearted, to proclaim liberty to the captives, and the opening of the prison to them that are bound; To proclaim the acceptable year of the Lord, and the day of vengeance of our God, to comfort all that mourn; To appoint unto them that mourn in Zion to give unto them BEAUTY FOR ASHES, the oil of joy for mourning, the garment of praise for the spirit of heaviness, that they might be called trees of righteousness, the planting of the Lord that he might be glorified (Isa. 61:1-3).

If He promised beauty for ashes, then He had foreknowledge that we would be "burnt" in life. If there were no burnings, there would be no ashes. If all was beautiful there would be no need for the exchange of ashes for beauty. When sin entered the Garden of Eden, it not only ushered in a change of lifestyle for Adam and Eve, it ushered in the ugliness of life — the sordid, bitter, and corrupt.

Life's bitterness needs to be sweetened with love, for love is the sweetener of the mind and body. Only God is pure love and to know Him is to travel the road that leads to higher heights above the smoke of disillusionment. The road of love will instruct how to clean out the ashes from hurtful experiences. It is important that one does not become a slave to the ugliness of the sin that became Adam and Eve's curse.

Determine to not live in the ashes. Rise up and become more Christ-like as you lean against Him. Let His Spirit infuse you with new strength and determination to build again things of lasting value. It is time to wake up and see that the hurtful things do not need to stop your life. You can go forward again.

Once more the prophet Isaiah gives hope, "Awake, awake; put on thy strength; put on thy beautiful garments, shake thyself from the dust" (Isa. 52:1-2).

Two things stand out to me in those verses. Number one, put on thy beautiful garments; and number two, shake thyself awake out of the stupor of heartache and despair. When your life has been charred and blackened by the blaze of injustice try to see the stars of hope as they beckon you to greater things.

Even mistakes can become masterpieces.

What was once termed Australia's biggest "mistake" was later hailed as its greatest — although costly — masterpiece. It was the Sydney Opera House. The original cost estimate announced in 1957 was $7.2 million. The final cost in 1973 reached $110 million. Concerning this unique structure, the state premier of New South Wales said: "The cost has become a secondary consideration to the perfection of the achievement."[2]

Let sorrow carve greatness in your soul. Arise a stately vessel of honor and beauty showing forth the work of the Architect, Jesus Christ.

Beauty is found in many things. One writer says beauty is in the eye of the beholder. We all know what beauty is when we see it. It has a feel about it. It is not associated with sordidness, but with freshness and wonderment. The poet Ralph Waldo Emerson says, "Never lose an opportunity of seeing anything that is beautiful, for beauty is God's handwriting — a wayside sacrament. Welcome it in every fair face, in every fair sky, in every flower, and thank God for it as a cup of blessing."[3]

Beauty is around us, but sometimes our heartaches blind us from seeing it. It can be seen in squalor as a tiny bud of a flower bursts forth with a sign of new hope even in a place of degradation. It is with effort sometimes that we bring ourselves to accept the beauty that is given to us.

Cecil, the philosopher, said, "Every year of my life I grow more convinced that it is wisest and best to fix our attention on the beautiful and the good, and dwell as little as possible on the evil and the false."[4]

Focus on truth and you will find beauty. Jesus said, "I am the way, the truth, and the life . . ." (John 14:6). He will lead you into beauty of heart, mind, and spirit. He can give beauty even in marred relationships.

It was Socrates that said, "I pray God, that I might be beautiful within." If you have inner beauty, you can pass through the squalor of the unclean and keep yourself clean. You will have the odors of the unclean situation cling to your outer garments, but the inner man, though wounded, can remain free of the disease of hate or bitterness. Open your eyes today to beauty and quit looking at the squalor and filth.

Bill Gaither, the song writer, wrote this beautiful song:

Something beautiful, something good.
All my confusion, Jesus understood.
All I have to offer him is brokenness and
      strife,
But He made something beautiful of my
      life.

If you have trouble seeing any beauty at all, and nothing looks good, ask the Lord to heal your spiritual heart and eyesight. For, "He hath made every thing beautiful in his time" (Eccles. 3:11). Whatever His hands touch becomes a thing of beauty. All you need is the touch of the Master's hand.

10

GOD'S FIRE

God's fire has a positive effect. You do not get burned with His fire. You only receive new power, strength, and vigor. Not all fire is a negative force. Fire can be used to make the world a better place to live. Wood stoves can help heat houses. A fire in the boiler of a boat or train will produce energy to propel it forward. Without fire we would be miserable. Many generations have sustained life by cooking with fire.

God's fire will help heal the wounds of the enemy's fire. God's fire can eat up the enemy's fire, for His power is more potent than the power of the enemy. This was proven when Moses and Aaron went before King Pharaoh and told him to let the people of God go free from the oppression of the Egyptians. Aaron threw his rod down and it became a serpent. King Pharaoh then called his wise men and the sorcerers in and they threw their rods down and they all became serpents; but Aaron's serpent swallowed up their serpents. It does not matter if it is a serpent or a fiery trial, God's fire can give you power to overcome or walk through the trial with victory.

Fire has been associated with God from the beginning of time. When Moses led the Israelites out from the land of Egypt, God used fire to help guide them. "And the Lord went before them by day in a pillar of a cloud to lead them the way; and by night in a pillar by fire, to give them light; to go by day and night" (Exod. 13:21).

He appeared to Moses on Mount Sinai in a blaze of fire. "And Mount Sinai was altogether on a smoke, because the Lord descended upon it in fire . . ." (Exod. 19:18).

Offerings were made with fire year after year and were part of the Judean religious customs instituted by God. "And the other lamb thou shalt offer at even . . . an offering made by fire unto the Lord" (Exod. 29:41).

"Then shall he bring it to the priest, and the priest shall take his handful of it . . . and burn on the altar, according to the offerings made by fire unto the Lord" (Lev. 5:12).

Somewhere in the midst of all the sin offerings, burnt offerings, and altars of incense, there came an awesome change. God decided to send fire to the people instead of the people sending fire up to Him in the form of altars of sacrifice.

He took the Law by the hand and walked it out of their lives by ushering in grace. When Jesus came to this world, not to condemn it but to save it, He did away with all the rituals of the tabernacle and Jewish tradition.

He told them the tabernacle was now in their heart, and they no longer had to go through the priest to get to God, but that they could come boldly to the throne of grace and be heard. He changed everything. This did not set well with some of the religious leaders and they decided to kill Him.

When Jesus first came, John the Baptist made a prophetic statement about Jesus and His mission. "John answered saying unto them all, I indeed baptize you with water; but one mightier than I cometh, the latchet of whose shoes I am not worthy to unloose: he shall baptize you with the HOLY GHOST AND WITH FIRE" (Luke 3:16).

This fire was to give power; for when Jesus had risen from the dead and was ascending into heaven, He told them this: "But ye shall receive power, after that the Holy Ghost is come upon you" (Acts 1:8).

The difference between God's fire and the enemy's fire is the end result. God's fire is to give you power to overcome; whereas the enemy's fire is to destroy you and leave you helpless. These two fires cannot even be compared because there is no comparison between them. It is like trying to compare a lump of clay to the most prized diamond.

The fire of the Old Testament associated with the Law is now the fire of the New Testament associated with grace. The two fires of God that give life and power are the Word and His Spirit.

John said, "He shall baptize you with the Holy Ghost and fire." The old prophet speaks about the Word being like a fire. "Is not my word like as a fire? saith the Lord" (Jer. 23:29).

The two New Testament fires (the Word and the Spirit) can quench the enemy's fire every time if allowed to do so.

How can the Spirit of God and the Word of God help you through difficulties and times of severe hurts and burnings? The Holy Spirit is a comforter. "But the Comforter, which is the Holy Ghost, whom the Father will send in my name, he shall teach you all things, and bring all things to your remembrance" (John 14:26).

Agnus Benigus Sanrey, a French theologian, wrote a ponderous volume entitled *Paracletus seu de recta pronunciations tractatus* in the seventeenth century — for the sole purpose of establishing the correct pronunciation of one word "Paracletus" translated as the "Comforter" in the Bible. Such a simple word, but a powerful one that merited someone writing volumes about.

COMFORTER — HIS SPIRIT

God's spirit is with you not only to give you power to be an overcomer and to witness to others, but to help you in your times of sorrow, disappointments, and hurts. He is your comfort and He is the supplier of those things which you need. He does care about all your problems, whether they are hurts or needs, as the following story demonstrates:

Years ago, the Free Kirk of Scotland was holding a meeting in the granite city of Aberdeen and worshippers were flocking in from all nearby towns to participate in the services. An aged man was wending his way to the city on foot, when he was overtaken by a young theological student; the two walked on in company. Despite the difference in their ages, they had much in common, and so they enjoyed chatting together as they jogged on toward their intended goal.

At noontime they turned aside to a grassy copse and sat down to eat the lunch which each had brought with him, first giving God thanks for His gracious provision. Afterwards the aged pilgrim suggested that they pray together before continuing their journey. The young theologian was a bit embarrassed, but agreed, intimating that the elder man should pray first, which he did. Addressing God as His Father in all simplicity, he poured out his heart in thanksgiving, then uttered three specific requests: he reminded the Lord that he was very hard of hearing and if he did not get a seat well up to the front in the kirk he would get little out of the sermon that evening, so he asked that a seat be kept for him near enough to the pulpit so he could get the benefit of the message. Secondly, he told the Lord that his shoes were badly worn and not fit for city streets. He pleaded for a new pair though he had not the money to purchase them. Last of all, he asked for a place to stay for the night, as he knew no one in Aberdeen and did not know where to look for accommodations.

By this time the student's eyes were wide open as he looked upon the old man with mingled disgust and amazement, thinking it the height of impertinence to burden the Deity with such trivialities. When his turn came to pray, he delivered himself of an eloquent, carefully composed discourse, which in turn amazed his older companion, who saw in it nothing that indicated a making known of his needs to God the Father.

Proceeding on their way, they reached the kirk just as the people were crowding in; it was soon evident that there was no longer even standing room left. The student thought, *Now we shall see what becomes of his presumptuous prayers. He'll see that God has more to do than to use His time saving a seat for a poor, old, country man.* However, someone came out and the old man was just able to squeeze inside the door, where he stood with his hand up to his ear trying to hear what was going on.

Just then, it happened that a young lady in a front pew turned and saw him. She called a sexton and said, "My father told me to hold our pew for him until time for the sermon; then, if he did not get here, to give it to someone else. Evidently, he has been detained. Will you please go back and bring up that old man who has his hand to his ear and is standing just inside the door?" In a few moments, petition number one was fully answered.

Now in Scotland, some folks always kneel for prayer as the minister leads, others reverently rise to their feet. The old man was the kneeling kind and the young woman always stood. As she looked down, she could not help observing the worn soles on the feet of the kneeling worshipper. Her father was a shoe-dealer! At the close of the service, she delicately approached the subject of the need of a better pair of shoes, and asked if she might take him to her father's store, though closed for the night, and present him with a pair. Needless to say, her offer was accepted as graciously as it was made. So petition number two was answered.

At the store the lady inquired where he was to stay for the night. In all simplicity he answered, "I dinna ken yet. My Father has a room for me, but He has no' told me what it is."

Puzzled for a moment, she exclaimed, "O, you mean your Father — God! Well, I believe we have that room for you. We were saving our guest room for the Rev. Dr. Blank, but a telegram came this morning saying he could not come, so now you must just come home with me and be our guest." And so the third petition was granted.

The next day the student inquired as to the outcome of the prayer and was astonished to find that God had heard and answered each particular plea.[1]

God not only hears your every prayer, He wants to hear them. He wants to be your comforter. His Spirit is not the only thing that will help you in your time of distress, but he gives you His word which is a lamp in the midnights of your life. Not only is it a light or a lamp, but it is the:

SWORD OF THE SPIRIT WHICH IS THE WORD OF GOD.

Ephesians gives all the proper pieces of armor to fight what? "Above all, taking the shield of faith, wherewith ye shall be able to quench all the fiery darts of the wicked, And take the helmet of salvation, and the sword of the Spirit, which is the word of God" (Eph. 6:16-17).

To fight off the FIERY darts of the wicked. Notice two things: The enemy only has darts, you have the Sword of Fire. Jeremiah likened the Word of God to a fire.

Can you get the picture? God's Spirit inside you, burning like a fire, and God's Word coming into your mind burning out thoughts that exalt themselves against the knowledge of God! Fire inside you, and when you quote the Scriptures, fire coming out of your mouth.

The crux of the matter is that you can take advantage of His Word and Spirit, or you can look at them, admire them, but never use them. It is like the young theologian and the old man. The young man knew about God, but the old man knew God.

God's "fire" is available to whosoever will, but it must be partaken of to realize the benefit. God's fire brings power, new ardor, and passion for living. It will kindle a flame in you that will invigorate and enthuse, instead of stifling and demolishing you.

11

BANKING THE FIRE

When we tried unsuccessfully to build a fire that cold winter day, the ashes were banked up about six inches deep. They had become hardened in spots and were in the way of any circulation of air. The ashes of yesterday's fire became a hindrance to the fire we were trying to build today.

The banking of ashes and building of shrines from the ashes are two different things, although they are both hindrances to a new constructive fire being built. Ashes that are left to pile up become meshed together and block out the needed circulation to build a good fire.

In the Old Testament it was required to dump the ashes from the fire that burned daily on the altar in the tabernacle. The ashes that can develop in God's fire can be many things. Two things that could be considered a hindrance in keeping a positive fire from burning are pride and prayerlessness.

1. **PRIDE** — thinking we are strong enough to

make it on our own, strong enough to make it on yesterday's fire, or when the fire is hot and we are feeling His power we start thinking it is our own power that is working in us.

This kind of thinking got a king into trouble once.

All this came upon the king Nebuchad-nezzar. At the end of twelve months he walked in the palace of the kingdom of Babylon. The king spake, and said, Is not this great Babylon, that I have built for the house of the kingdom by the might of my power, and for the honour of my majesty? While the word was in the king's mouth, there fell a voice from heaven, saying, O king Nebuchad-nezzar, to thee it is spoken, The kingdom is departed from thee. And they shall drive thee from men, and thy dwelling shall be with the beasts of the field; they shall make thee to eat grass as oxen and seven times shall pass over thee, until thou know that the most High ruleth in the kingdom of men, and giveth it to whomsoever he will (Dan. 4:28-32).

The very same hour that he spoke, he also was driven from the kingdom and into the field. There he ate grass as an oxen and his body was wet with the dew of the heaven until his hairs were grown like eagles' feathers, and his nails like birds' claws.

At the end of the time God had set his punishment to be, his understanding returned to him and he blessed the most High and praised and honored Him. He gave quite a speech after eating, having had nothing to eat but grass and wandering about like an animal.

He said, "And all the inhabitants of the earth are reputed as nothing: and he doeth according to his will in the army of heaven, and among the inhabitants of the earth: and none can stay his hand, or say unto him, What doest thou?

"Now I Nebuchadnezzar praise and extol and honour the King of heaven, all whose works are truth, and his ways judgment: and those that walk in pride he is able to abase" (Dan. 4:35,37).

It is amazing how we learn from humbling experiences. When we are lifted up by the light of our own importance, we become blinded to solid truth. Because of pride, Nebuchadnezzar could not see the glory of God and His majesty. His own feelings of self-importance superseded the eternal truth that man cannot make it successfully without God helping him.

When God gives us the fire of His Spirit, it will burn out the dross of bitterness, anger, and self-importance and we will become a new creature in Christ. As we walk in Christ we must always remember that it is the fire of His love and His Spirit that gives us the power to overcome and to minister to others effectively.

Let us always be aware of the hard lesson Nebuchadnezzar learned and give God the glory due Him. Knowing fully that it is He that gives us breath to breathe naturally and spiritually. Acts 17:28 says it well, "For in him we live, and move, and have our being."

2. PRAYERLESSNESS — is caused by a feeling of self-sufficiency. It is also sometimes a result of a lack of discipline on our part to do what we know to be right.

The fire of God's Spirit was initiated by prayer. Prayer was made and salvation came. The only way to keep that fire burning is to build a fresh altar of prayer every day. When a prayerless spirit grips us, we are advocating that we are strong in our own might and we do not have to plug in to the Source of power. The ashes of yesterday's prayers combined with the ashes of pride stack up until beginning a new prayer becomes difficult.

It becomes needful to clean out the banked ashes and just start communicating with God all over again. Jesus said in Luke 18:1, "Men ought always to pray and not to faint." A prayerless life will cause you to faint, and make your fire flicker and go out.

Prayer is the most powerful thing you can do. When you pray you communicate with God and God owns all power. Prayer stiffens the purpose, gives you insight and inspiration. It links you with divinity and takes you from the lowlands of mediocrity to excellence. It gives wisdom, grace, and understanding. It is the one thing that will change situations from worse to better.

Dr. Alexis Carrel is a medical doctor who won a Nobel Prize in physiology. He wrote: "Prayer is the most powerful form of energy that one can generate. The influence of prayer on the human mind and body is as demonstrable as that of secreting glands. Its results can be measured in terms of increased buoyancy, greater intellectual vigor, moral stamina, and a deeper understanding of human relationships.

"Prayer is indispensable to the fullest development of personality. Only in prayer do we achieve that complete harmonious assembly of mind, body, and spirit, which gives the frail human need its unshakable strength."[1]

It was Tennyson who said, "More things are wrought by prayer than this world dreams of." It is necessary that we realize the importance of prayer so we do not become victims of prayerlessness.

There are prayers and then there are prayers. This was the case of Colonel Gracie's wife. It was a Sunday night in April 1912. She started to go to bed, but a heavy burden gripped her and she kneeled down to prayer. She prayed with tremendous earnestness for her husband who was on the *Titanic* somewhere in the mid-Atlantic. As the hours went by she could get no assurance and kept praying in agony until about five o'clock in the morning when a great peace washed over her and she slept.

Meanwhile her husband was among the doomed hundreds who were trying frantically to launch the lifeboats from the ship which had struck an iceberg. He had given up all hope of saving himself and was trying to help the women and children.

As the ship plunged to her watery grave, he was sucked down in the giant whirlpool. He began to swim under the ice-cold water, praying in his heart. Suddenly he came to the surface and found himself near an overturned lifeboat. Along with several others he climbed aboard, and was picked up by another lifeboat about five in the morning. Because a woman in America prayed **until** she knew everything was all right, God intervened and took care of her husband out in the ocean.

These are not the only things that make it difficult to get a good hot fire going. You know what it is that hinders you from being able to let the breath of God's Spirit flow through you so a hot fire can be kindled. It was Wesley who said, "If I had three hundred men who feared nothing but God, hated nothing but sin, and were determined to know nothing among men but Jesus Christ and Him crucified, I would set the world on fire."[2]

Christ is looking for hot hearts to do His mission on earth. Banked ashes can keep the Church from burning with the fire of zeal — zeal which will take average men and women and make them do impossible things.

12

CLEANING OUT THE ASHES

Every day you need to clean out the ashes from yesterday's fire. Your spirit can become bitter and affect others around you, or it can become better and do the same. Whether you clean out the ashes or not, they still affect all you meet.

> The spirit of a man looks out through the eyes and flings its light on the face and hangs upon the form its own subtle drapery. It walks forth and lays hold of the spirits of others and imparts its good or evil. Whether one wills or not, so it does."[1]

It is not always easy to clean out the ashes, but with courage you can do it! I will never forget the Scripture God gave me while I was riding on a plane en route to help mend a broken relationship. It was in Numbers 13:20. Moses was talking to the twelve spies before he sent them out on their venture and he said these words, "Be of good courage."

Courage is the heart, mind, spirit, temper or disposition, desire, will, or intention. It is that quality of mind which enables one to encounter danger and difficulties with firmness, valor, and bravery.

Encourage means to give courage to; or inspire with courage, spirit or hope, and to raise the confidence of someone. Discourage means to lessen the courage of; to dishearten, to depress the spirits, and to deprive of confidence.

The devil, according to legend, once advertised his tools for sale at a public auction. When the prospective buyers assembled, there was one oddly shaped tool which was labeled, "Not for sale." Asked to explain why this was, the devil answered, "I can spare my other tools, but I cannot spare this one. It is the most useful implement that I have. It is called discouragement, and with it I can work my way into hearts otherwise inaccessible. When I get this tool into a man's heart, the way is open to plant anything there I desire."

Be encouraged in cleaning out the ashes, building again, and living with hope once more. The Bible says:

THEY ENCOURAGED THEMSELVES
(Judg. 20:12)

DAVID ENCOURAGED HIMSELF
(1 Sam. 30:6)

THEY ENCOURAGED ONE ANOTHER
(Isa. 41:7).

We learn from the successes and failures of others. Isaiah 41:6 gives us insight on how to act with one another while going through difficult times. "They helped everyone his neighbour; and everyone said to his brother, "BE OF GOOD COURAGE." Times may be tough, but be of good courage. Be brave in the face of difficulties. Stand strong in the day of adversity and you will survive and win.

How do you encourage yourself? Second Chronicles 31:4 tells us that they were encouraged by the law of the Lord. If you will get a hold of the Word of God and devour it daily, memorize it, and meditate upon it, you are promised success and blessing. This type of power cannot be equaled. The written Word becomes alive in your soul, mind, and heart, enabling you to meet the most formidable situation and overcome it.

Courage consists not of blindly overlooking danger or difficult situations, but in seeing it and conquering it. Courage is grace under pressure. When the pressure of broken relationships comes, "Be strong and of good courage . . . be not afraid, neither be thou dismayed: for the Lord thy God is with thee withersoever thou goest" (Josh. 1:6,9).

When hard times come, take courage and find the jewel of truth, hope, and opportunity in the rubble of despair. Ann Landers was asked if there was one predominant problem that people had over others. She said the problem was FEAR — fear of losing their health, wealth, or loved ones through death or a broken relationship. She said, "People are afraid of life itself. They seem to have lost their courage."

You have to work on strengthening your will. Will yourself to not be afraid. When the angel appeared to Hagar during her time of a broken relationship, he said, "Fear not, for God hath heard" (Gen. 21:17). You cannot lay down and die inside yourself;

you must keep courage and live again. Say every day, "The Lord is on my side; I will not fear: what can man do unto me?" (Ps. 118:6). Courage is not a brilliant dash or a dazzling light that flashes and passes away from sight. It is an unwavering trait that has the patience to wait.

When Elisha and his servant were surrounded by the enemy and the servant's heart became fearful, Elisha said these words, "Fear not! They that be with us are more than they that be with them" (2 Kings 6:16). If God is on your side, what else do you need? He is all powerful and can help you through the most difficult period of your life.

There is an interesting account in the Old Testament that proves God will help you in difficult situations if you will lean on Him and be courageous in the battle. Kings Jeroboam and Abijah went to war in 2 Chronicles 13. King Abijah set the battle in array with an army of valiant men of war; four hundred thousand chosen men. King Jeroboam also brought against him eight hundred thousand chosen men of valor.

When the two armies met near Mount Zemaraim, King Abijah stood up on the mountain and gave a speech. He said, "Hear me, thou Jeroboam, and all Israel; Ought ye not to know that the Lord God of Israel gave the kingdom over Israel to David for ever, even to him and to his sons by a covenant of salt? Yet Jeroboam the son of Nebat, the servant of Solomon the son of David, is risen up, and hath rebelled against his lord" (2 Chron. 13:4-6).

He went on to give a little history of what led up to the war and brought to the people's attention that Jeroboam had rebelled against the Lord and made gods of golden calves. He said, "But as for us, the Lord is our God, and we have not forsaken him; and the priests, which minister unto the Lord, are the sons of Aaron, and the Levites wait upon their business: And they burn unto the Lord every morning and every evening burnt sacrifices and sweet incense . . . for we keep the charge of the Lord our God; but ye have forsaken him. And, behold, God himself is with us for our captain. . . . O children of Israel, fight ye not against the Lord God of your fathers; for ye shall not prosper" (2 Chron. 13:10-12).

While the king was talking, the other king caused an ambush to come from behind them and also before them. When Judah looked back "they cried unto the Lord, and the priests sounded with the trumpets" (2 Chron. 13:14). Then they gave a shout! As they shouted, it came to pass that God smote Jeroboam and all Israel before Abijah and Judah. Here is the key: "The children of Judah prevailed, because they **relied upon the Lord God of their fathers**" (2 Chron. 13:18).

It does not matter if the enemy looks like he has you outnumbered. King Abijah only had four hundred thousand men while King Jeroboam had eight hundred thousand men. God does not need numerical strength to do a miracle, he only needs trust in Him. He has all the power in the world. "If God be for you, who can be against you?" (Rom. 8:31).

Do not be of good courage in yourself, but rely upon the strength of God and He will help you. If you do not have the courage, "Wait on the Lord: be of good courage, and he shall strengthen thine heart: wait, I say, on the Lord" (Ps. 27:14). Never give up.

Cleaning out the ashes requires patience. When I clean the ashes out of our wood fireplace, it takes time because the ashes tend to fly around. They have to be handled with diligence and care. They have to be picked up very carefully with the shovel and placed in the container to be used to dump the ashes.

This is applicable with the ashes of our own lives. Patience and diligence are required to clean them out properly. Careful consideration of the job at hand is necessary so the ashes will not fly in all directions and settle on things of value. Place the ashes in the container that was provided for them to be put in and then go dump them.

It is like a statement I heard one time: "There is plenty of room at the top, but there is no elevator in the building." There is plenty of room to get rid of the ashes, but it is a chore to do so. Make up your mind that you are going to do it and then start working on it with patience, courage, and diligence. Clean out everything that does not glorify God and that pulls you down. It is time to be honest, no matter which way things go.

The story was told of a slave auction in one of the southern states many years ago. A smart, active boy was put up for sale. A kind master who had compassion on him, wishing him not to have a cruel owner, went up to him, and said, "If I buy you, will you be honest?"

The boy, with a look that baffled description, replied, "I will be honest whether you buy me or not."

This is essential for healing — honesty with yourself and God no matter who is involved, or what is pending. God can turn any situation around, but He honors honesty. Do not leave some of the ashes piled around inside your heart, clean them all the way out.

13

RECOVERY FROM BURNS

When a burn victim is rushed to the hospital and doctors and nurses begin to work on the damage done by the fire, it is just the beginning of a process. The burning itself did not take long; it is the painful months afterwards which are difficult for the patient. Recovery takes time, patience, and discipline. It is a time of restoration from ill health to good health, marred skin to good skin.

Unless you experience a miracle of instant healing, as some do, your emotional hurt will take time to heal. It is a time to, "Trust in the Lord with all thine heart; and lean not unto thine own understanding" (Prov. 3:5). It is a time to establish your heart and fix it on God, because the thing that it was fixed on before let you down. Everything else may fail, but God never fails.

The hardest thing to do is wait or be still. This is a generation that demands everything in a hurry and if it is not delivered within a few minutes, countenances become tense and angry, fingers start tapping on the table, and a slow volcano starts to flow inside the heart. All because of the hurry syndrome that the modern generation has developed.

Instant coffee, instant hot water, instant banking, instant credit, and instant drive-ins have influenced the Christian to be tempted to expect instant answers. Sometimes God answers instantly when we call, other times He makes us wait — but He is always faithful. In your recovery, be patient and confident. The Lord will help you if you allow Him to be God. "Cast not away therefore your confidence, which hath great recompense of reward. For ye have need of patience, that after ye have done the will of God, ye might receive the promise" (Heb. 10:35-36).

There is strength in waiting. Isaiah describes it well. "But they that wait upon the Lord shall renew their strength; they shall mount up with wings as eagles; they shall run, and not be weary; and they shall walk, and not faint" (Isa. 40:31). How? By waiting on the Lord. There is a time to run, and there is a time to be still. When you are recovering, you need those daily "still" times with the Master. "Be still, and know that I am God" (Ps. 46:10).

> Not so in haste, my heart!
> Have faith in God and wait;
> Although He linger long,
> He never comes too late.[1]

It has been said, "Patience is bitter, but its fruits sweet."

When the great St. Gothard Tunnel was being constructed, workmen bore simultaneously from either side of the Alps. For nearly ten years they worked in the dark; but in 1881, one of the parties of workman began to hear, through the lessening thickness of intervening rocks, the sounds of the hammers and the voices of the workmen from the other side. On they worked, listening, working; working, listening. One day they broke down the barrier between them. Men rushed from the other side, grasped hands, and looked excitedly into each other's faces, giving whoops and shouts of joy. They had finally accomplished their mission.

You may feel like you are in a dark tunnel and cannot get out, but if you keep boring through in prayer and faith God will break down the wall and the light will shine through the tunnel. Barriers will be gone and you and God will be victorious because you never gave up on God.

In 1986, when we were going through a deep trial, God spoke the following Scripture to me very forcibly while sitting in a church service. I dated it, Wednesday, October 29, 1986, and in big letters wrote, **GOD'S IN CHARGE**. "Sit still, my daughter, until thou know how the matter will fall" (Ruth 3:18).

The story of Ruth could not have been written without Naomi, her mother-in-law. Naomi and her husband, Elimelech, were God-fearing people who lived in Jerusalem until a famine came. They decided to move out of Jerusalem and go to Moab. (Be careful what you do during famine.) This was a wrong move on their part as you see the story unfold, but it is a story of life, with its imperfections, mistakes, and wrong judgment.

Naomi tasted the cup of bitterness so much that when she returned to Bethlehem and her friends saw her, they said, "Is this Naomi?" They could not believe their eyes. She answered them out of a sorrowful heart, "Call me not Naomi, call me Mara: for the Almighty hath dealt very bitterly with me. I went out full, and the Lord hath brought me home again empty: why then call ye me Naomi, seeing the Lord hath testified against me, and the Almighty hath afflicted me" (Ruth 1:20-21).

Naomi started out in life with joy, hope, and promise. Her name means, "my joy," "my bliss," or "pleasantness of Jehovah," and is a name suggestive of all that is charming, agreeable, and attractive. Something happened along the way that changed her for awhile, for the story does end well.

During the time of the Judges, Israel suffered a very serious famine which was considered to be one of the punishments visited upon the people when they had sinned. Elimelech, the Ephrathite of Bethlehem, decided to emigrate with his family to another place where food was more plentiful. In taking the initiative to go to Moab, a foreign heathen country, Naomi's husband stepped out of the will of God. One writer said that if the famine came as a punishment from God, Elimelech should have repented, tried to help his fellow countrymen back to God, and prayed for the removal of the scourge.

Elimelech was a Hebrew, and so he had the promise given them. "In the days of famine, thou shalt be satisfied."

Elimelech means, "My God is King." If he really believed that God was King, would not he have trusted Him in the bad times? It was not long after they left Moab that Naomi and Elimelech started having doubts about their decision. Things went from bad to worse over the years. The Jewish law forbade marriage outside of the nation of Israel, but their two sons married Moabite women.

Sorrow started to dog Naomi's footsteps. Her husband, who had taken her to a land where there seemed to be more, died even where there was lots of food, leaving her a widow. Then her two sons died. Her whole family was gone and she was in a strange land, not the land of her roots and people. She had nothing left except two daughters-in-law. When she told them she was going back to Bethlehem, Orpah kissed her mother-in-law good-bye. Then Naomi turned to Ruth and said, "Behold, thy sister-in-law is gone back unto her people, and unto her gods: return thou after thy sister-in-law" (Ruth 1:15). Ruth passionately cried these immortal words as she clave to Naomi. "Intreat me not to leave thee, or to return from following after thee: for whither thou goest, I will go; and where thou lodgest, I will lodge: thy people shall be my people, and thy God my God: Where thou diest, will I die, and there will I be buried: the Lord do so to me, and more also, if ought but death part thee and me" (Ruth 1:16-17).

Ruth saw that Naomi had something more than she did. There was a steadfast faith Naomi had that Ruth wanted. She realized that her gods were ineffective and could not help her during her sorrow. There was a determination in her that shone through to Naomi. Naomi sensed the hunger and desire, "When she saw that she was steadfastly minded to go with her, then she left speaking unto her" (Ruth 1:18). She did not try to change Ruth's mind, she accepted it as the will of God. So the two lonely widows traveled together down a long dusty road to Bethlehem.

When they entered the city their appearance there caused quite a stir. The people were shocked, and voiced their shock. Naomi, who once was so sweet, was now more sour, and blamed God for the poverty and desolation she had endured. The cup of bitterness she was partaking of was not an act of God, but a result of disobedience. She left full, but returned empty.

When there is a "burning" in your life, be careful not to charge God foolishly. Hurtful experiences are orchestrated by several things. First of all, the devil orchestrates evil, as in the case of Job. He is out to hurt you. Second, our own disobedience causes a ramification of evil. There is the law of the harvest, first the sowing, then the reaping. Third, you can make a poor judgment call. A lack of wisdom can thrust you into a situation that you were not expecting or prepared to face. Fourth, you can experience evil by being a victim of circumstances. Example: A drunken father, speeding down the highway, has an accident and kills his little girl. The little girl was innocent, but the father's wrong orchestrated evil.

Whether your "burn" came from the devil, disobedience, poor judgment, or another's wrongdoing, in your time of recovery, learn to be still with your tongue and in your spirit and seek to know God. Say with Job, "Naked came I out of my mother's womb, and naked shall I return thither: the Lord gave, and the Lord hath taken away; blessed be the name of the Lord" (Job 1:21). "Though he slay me, yet will I trust in him" (Job 13:15).

There is a good ending to the story of Ruth and Naomi. Remember, with God things always get better. In Bethlehem, Naomi had a kinsman of her husband's, a mighty man of wealth, whose name was Boaz. God helped them out of their affliction. Boaz married Ruth and from this union a baby was born named Obed, the father of Jesse, the father of David. Boaz and Ruth took care of Naomi the rest of her days, and she became a rich woman again: rich in friends, rich in grandchildren, rich in God, and rich in spirit. The recovery was long and painful, but the restoration came.

Professor R.G. Moulton expressed it this way. "The family she thought she had seen perish has been restored to the genealogies of Israel; for baby Obed lives to become the father of Jesse, and Jesse is father of the great King David. And in the genealogical tables of Matthew, the Moabite who left her people for love is Naomi, duly named as an ancestor of the Messiah himself."[2]

What looks like a disaster can be turned into something rich and good when God becomes involved with it. "Man's extremities are God's opportunities." The secret is to relax, wait, be confident in God, and let go. If you clutch your problem tightly to your bosom until it permeates your whole being, you are not letting God work.

In North Africa the natives have a very easy way to capture monkeys. A gourd, with a hole just sufficiently large so that a monkey can put his hand into it, is filled with nuts and fastened firmly to a branch of a tree in the evening time. During the night a monkey will smell the food, go to the source of it, put his hand down inside the gourd, and grasp a handful of nuts. The hole is too small for the monkey to withdraw his clenched fist, and he does not have the sense to let go. He pulls and pulls all night long, until he is captured in the morning.

Jesus said, "Come unto me, all ye that labour and are heavy laden, and I will give you rest. Take my yoke upon you, and learn of me; for I am meek and lowly in heart: and ye shall find rest unto your souls. For my yoke is easy, and my burden is light" (Matt. 11:28-30). Let go and let God. He said in Isaiah 43:13, "Yea, before the day was I am he; and there is none that can deliver out of my hand: I will work, and who shall let it?" Let God help you recover from the hurtful things in life. He never makes mistakes. He will heal your inner hurts and give you a song again. Do not keep one smidgen of your problem inside you. Give it all to God.

R.G. le Tourneau, the earthmoving machinery manufacturer who died in 1969, failed often in the earlier years of his career. During the years of the Depression, he made $35,000 profit in one year, which surprised everyone. Puffed up with pride, he withheld the payment of his $5,000 annual pledge to the Lord in order to reinvest it in his business, which he said he wanted to use so he could have a greater share the following year. He anticipated a net profit of $100,000.

Within a year his anticipated $100,000 profit was turned into a $100,000 loss, which brought le Tourneau to his knees. While praying in repentance he told God he would pay $5,000 the following year and also $5,000 for the year he missed. This is when he was flat broke and several employees were threatening to leave him.

From that point on le Tourneau's fortune changed, and within four years he and his wife founded the le Tourneau Foundation comprised of 90 percent of the stocks of le Tourneau Corporation, the earnings of which financed evangelical Christian work worldwide. At one point, this foundation was worth $40 million.

The point in all of this is what le Tourneau said: "It is not how much money I give to God, but how much of God's money I keep for myself." I would like to re-word it and make it applicable to your problem. "It is not how much of your problem you give to God, it is how much of your problem you keep, that makes the difference."

In 1 Peter 5:6-7 it says, "Humble yourselves therefore under the mighty hand of God, that he may exalt you in due time: Casting all your care upon him; for he careth for you." Matthew Henry's comments on the "casting on the Lord" are rich and worth pondering. He says, "Throw your cares, which are so cutting and distracting, which wound your souls and pierce your hearts, upon the wise and gracious providence of God; trust in Him with a firm composed mind, for He careth for you. He is willing to release you of your care, and take the care of you upon himself. He will either avert what you fear, or support you under it. He will order all events to you so as shall convince you of His paternal love and tenderness towards you; and all shall be so ordered that no hurt, but good, shall come unto you."[3]

Maude Royden made a statement that is powerful: "When you have nothing left but God, then for the first time you become aware that God is enough." If you trust as a child and believe that God can do anything, then He will start doing great things for you. It is not enough to say, "Okay, I'll give it to God," and then worry about it all night until you are a nervous wreck. You take pills to pep you up and tranquilizers to make you sleep. Your fretfulness is seen in your face and in your actions. This defies your words. If you just release it, God will increase you and help you in your difficult dilemma.

Earl C. Willer shares the following inspirational story:

> Captain Johnson was serving as chaplain on an island in the South Pacific during

World War II. He prepared to go on a bombing raid on enemy-occupied islands several hundred miles away. The mission was a complete success, but on the homeward course the plane began to lose altitude and the engines faded out. A safe landing was made on a strange island. It was learned later that the enemy was just one-half mile in each direction, yet the landing had gone undetected.

The staff sergeant came to the chaplain and said, "Chaplain, you have been telling us for months of the need of praying and believing God answers prayer in time of trouble, and that He does it right away. We're out of gas and the base is several hundred miles away — almost surrounded by the enemy."

Johnson began to pray and lay hold of the promises, and believed that God would work a miracle. Night came and the chaplain continued in his intense prayer. About 2:00 a.m. the sergeant awakened and felt compelled to walk to the water's edge. He discovered a metal float which had drifted up on the beach — octane gas. In a few hours the crew reached their home base safely.

An investigation revealed that the skipper of a U.S. tanker, finding his ship in sub-infested waters, had his gasoline cargo removed so as to minimize the danger in case of a torpedo hit. Barrels were placed on barges and put adrift six hundred miles from where Johnson and the plane crew were forced down. God had navigated one of these barges through wind and current and beached it fifty steps from the stranded men.[4]

You say, "Well, that's them, not me. It always seems to happen for others." I challenge you to put your FULL trust in the Lord Jesus Christ and let Him take over and be completely in charge. He is able and He is faithful; He will not let you down! During the time of healing, let Him pour the oil into your wounds and they will heal so much faster. He will give you "the oil of joy for mourning" (Isa. 61:3). That is why He came. He is waiting to heal you, for He is the Great Physician.

14

THE REFINER'S FIRE

The Lord said, "Behold, I have refined thee, but not with silver; I have chosen thee in the furnace of affliction" (Isa. 48:10). To refine something means to reduce to a fine, unmixed, or pure state; to free from dross; to improve or perfect. Matthew Henry's comments are, "His dealings with the people were not to cut them off, but to do them good. It was to refine them, but not as silver, or with silver, not so thoroughly as men refine their silver, which they continue in the furnace till all the dross is separated from it; if God should take that course with them, they would be always in the furnace, for they are all dross, and, as such, might justly be put away."[1]

No one can read the history of God's ancient people without knowing the wonderful compassion of the Lord. Their numerous transgressions caused Him to deal with them often. Sometimes He dealt with them through the furnace of affliction. A furnace is prepared for gold so it can be refined; it makes it much purer than before. It melts the gold, and makes it soft before it is refined. The heat of the furnace will destroy tin and lead, and also the drossy part of gold.

When the fire is hot in your life, remember the gold process. Job said, "But he knoweth the way that I take: when he hath tried me, I shall come forth as gold" (Job 23:10). Metal is not worth much until it has been tempered by fire. Mankind is also tempered by the fire — it builds strength. Iron enters the soul and we are stronger and made ready for greater things.

The following story was found in a book that is over seventy years old.

> Seeking a deliverer and a Saviour, the great God in His own purpose passed by the palace, and its silken delights.
>
> He took a little babe in His arms and called to His side His favorite angel, the angel of sorrow.
>
> Stooping He whispered, "O Sorrow, thou well beloved teacher, take thou this child of mine and make him great.
>
> "Take him to yonder cabin in the wilderness; make his home a poor man's home; plant his narrow path thick with thorns; cut his little feet with sharp rocks as he climbs the hills with difficulty.
>
> "Make each footprint red with his own life blood; load his little back with burdens; give to him days of toil and nights of study and sleeplessness.
>
> "Wrest from his arms whatever he loves; make his heart, through sorrow, as sensitive to the sigh of a slave as a thread of silk in a window is sensitive to the slightest wind that

blows; and when you have digged lines of pain in his cheek and made his face more marred than the face of any man of his time, bring him back to me, and with him I will free 4,000,000 slaves."

That is how God made Abraham Lincoln.[2]

Sorrow is a teacher, but it is a painful one. It teaches one to be more sympathetic and compassionate. Sorrow humbles the soul and takes away the stiff pride that dwells in the haughty backbone. It tenderizes, and makes one more like Christ — forgiving instead of condemning, loving instead of hating.

The consolation is that Christ is with you in all your troubles, sorrows, trials, furnaces, and burnings. He does care. Tissot, the artist, planned to paint a picture with the title, *The Choir Singer*, as this was a popular thing for society women to be involved in, because it made them appear to be more religious. He went to a great church in Paris to study the setting for his picture, but into his soul came a vision altogether different from what he had planned.

He seemed to see the ruins of a large castle with windows and walls broken and shattered. In the debris sat a weary peasant and his wife, with a small bundle, their only earthly belongings, resting beside them. They were a picture of despair. While they sat, the artist saw in the vision a figure of a Man with bleeding hands and feet and a crown on His head. It was the Man of Sorrows. He sat beside the weeping pair, in order to console them.

When the artist returned to his studio, he tried to continue on the canvas he had planned, but constantly there came before him the vision of Christ showing compassion to the old couple. From that vision came his painting called, *Christ the Consoler*.

The fifty-third chapter of Isaiah describes the Lord Jesus Christ. "He is despised and rejected of men; a man of sorrows, and acquainted with grief....Surely he hath borne our griefs, and carried our sorrows: yet we did esteem him stricken.... But he was wounded for our transgressions, he was bruised for our iniquities" (Isa. 53:3-5).

Except for Christ's sorrows, there would be no redemption for the world. The rejection, misunderstanding, and envy He suffered at the hand of the religious leaders was all for a purpose. What if He would have been accepted and lived a life of ease? All great things are accomplished through the hot heat of sorrow. A heart is broken — then a song is born, a book is written, or a message is preached that will touch thousands of lives.

The best in a person is not discovered at a party or on beds of ease. It is the struggles of life that produce the gold.

The fire of the furnace is to make you better, or work something out in your life that is a negative factor.

Bernard Gilpin, accused of heresy before Bishop Bonner, set out for London for trial. His favorite saying was, "All things are for the best." On his journey, he broke his leg. "Is all for the best now?" jested a scorner.

"I still believe so," he answered.

And so it proved that he was right. Before he was able to resume his journey, Queen Mary died. Instead of going to London to be burned, he returned home in triumph. God does have His eyes upon you and is working things out for your good, if you will work with Him and not kick against His ways.

The great singer, Enrico Caruso, used to have a favorite expression: "Bisogna soffrire per essere grandi." The words mean, "To be great, it is necessary to suffer."

After years of difficulty, Caruso achieved fame; but he communicated more than beautiful music through his voice. A music critic observed, "His is a voice that loves you, but not only a voice, a sympathetic man." Tribulation does that for a person who accepts life's difficulties in the proper spirit.

One writer wrote, "Paul's sweetest epistles are from prison cells. John's Revelation was written in exile; Bunyan's *Pilgrim's Progress* came from the Bedford jail; Luther's translation of the German Bible was when he was shut in Wartburg Castle; Madam Guyon's sweetest poems and deepest experiences were from long imprisonments."

The writer of the Psalms expressed the principle that a time of affliction was good for a person. "Before I was afflicted I went astray: but now have I kept thy word . . . . It is good for me that I have been afflicted; that I might learn thy statutes" (Ps. 119:67,71).

Edward Young once stated:

Amid my list of blessings infinite,
Stands this the foremost,
That my heart has bled.

It has often been said, "You have to bleed to bless." Before Moses led, he bled. Before he bled, he was rash, unwise, and hotheaded. The banishment from the palace tempered him until God saw that he was ready to be the leader for the deliverance of the Israelites. What looked like defeat for Moses proved to be the very thing he needed to improve his character and judgment. God works things out for our good even when it looks like it is not.

W.W. Weeks shares the story of how a tragedy turned out to be a blessing in disguise. Years ago a fishing fleet went out from a small harbor on the east coast of Newfoundland. In the afternoon there came up a great storm. When night settled, not a single vessel of all the fleet had found its way into port. All night long wives, mothers, children, and sweethearts paced up and down the beach, wringing their hands and calling on God to save their loved ones. To add to the horror of the situation, one of the cottages caught fire. Since the men were all away, it was impossible to save the home.

When the morning came, to the joy of all, the entire fleet found safe harbor in the bay. But there was one face which was a picture of despair, the wife of the man whose home had been destroyed. Meeting her husband as he landed, she cried, "Oh, husband, we are ruined! Our home and all it contained was destroyed by fire!"

But the man exclaimed, "Thank God for the fire! It was the light of our burning cottage that guided the whole fleet into port!"

This is not to say that we should want to live in the fire, for if that were the case we would be consumed and die. We would not choose it, but if it comes, we will work with the Refiner, for He allowed it for our good. We must come forth as gold.

To be on the gold level, there must be a trying or refining process and that always involves fire. The fiery trials are for our glory. If we never cried, we would become hard and brittle. It is the tears that keep us soft and understanding.

You say, "But my situation has no gold in it. It is

all shame, degradation, abuse, and embarrassment. How could any good come out of such a mess?" The unique thing about Christ is that He specializes in bringing you up to a higher level of living. The lowest gutter is not too low for Him. The worst abuse does not have too much stigma. The filth and degradation is not too dirty for Him. If you can believe in Christ, He can make it better and give you a new heart. This is the miracle of Calvary. It does not make any difference to Christ whether it is a Christian or a sinner who is suffering. He can help whosoever will let Him. If you are a good person who suffers at the hand of an evil person remember Joseph. Good came for him and many others because he kept the right attitude.

Suffering will come. Let it refine you instead of making you bitter and brittle. Soft and pliable in the Master's hand, and yielding to His every command, is what He desires of His children. He would never allow you to be hurt just to be mean. He is too gentle and kind, merciful and loving. He only allows it so you can become more refined and get the "tin" or the "junk" out and make you more fruitful or productive.

The two following Scriptures need to be a part of your daily reading when you are going through the fire. They are:

> But the God of all grace, who hath called us unto his eternal glory by Christ Jesus, after that ye have suffered a while, make you perfect, stablish, strengthen, settle you (1 Pet. 5:10).

> Beloved, think it not strange concerning the fiery trial which is to try you, as though some strange thing happened to you: But rejoice, inasmuch as ye are partakers of

Christ's sufferings; that, when his glory shall be revealed, ye may be glad also with exceeding joy (1 Pet. 4:12-13).

15

HOT PRAYERS

Dr. Alexis Carrel made this statement, "As a physician, I have seen men, after all other therapy had failed, lifted out of disease and melancholy by the effort of prayer. When we address God in fervent prayer, we change both soul and body for the better."[1]

In 1935, Alexander Lake, author of the book, *Your Prayers Are Always Answered*,[2] did a survey at random in the city of Los Angeles. His question was, "Do you believe that spiritual healings — that is — physical and mental healings by faith in God alone, are possible?" These were his findings:

> Twenty-seven said: "Yes."
> Eleven said: "I don't know."
> Twelve said: "No."

Again in June 1955, he asked the same question of the same fifty Los Angeles doctors.

> Forty-seven said: "Yes."
> One said: "I don't know."
> Two said: "No."

Three of the twelve who said "no" in 1935, said "yes" in 1955. When he asked what had happened to change their minds, the three said, in effect: "We have learned that man's natural state is one of well-being; and that there is a spiritual entity in man that when activated by faith, destroys physical and mental illness."[3]

James 5:15-16 says, "The prayer of faith shall save the sick, and the Lord shall raise him up; and if he have committed sin, they shall be forgiven him. Confess your faults one to another, and pray one for another, that ye may be healed. The effectual fervent prayer of a righteous man availeth much."

It is the hot, fervent, desperate prayers that accomplish much. Once there was a little mother who had five children. She had been widowed during World War II. One night after surveying the bare food cupboard, she put the children to bed, and rocked the baby to sleep who was sick, praying all the while that the Lord would help her in her desperate hour.

The next morning she set out from her house on a mission. It was the week before Christmas and she went to a little grocery store on the west side of town. When she entered the store she went straight to the grocer and asked him for enough food to make up a Christmas dinner for her children. He asked her how much she could afford to spend.

She answered, "My husband was killed in the war, I have nothing to offer but a little prayer."

The man confessed later that he was not very sentimental in those days. A grocery store could not be run like a bread line. So he said, "Write it on paper," and turned about his business.

To his surprise, the woman plucked a piece of paper out of her bosom and handed it to him over the counter and said, "I did that during the night watching over my sick baby."

The grocer took the paper before he could recover from his surprise, and then regretted having done so! For what would he do with it? Then an idea suddenly came to him. He placed the paper, without even reading the prayer, on the weight side of his old-fashioned scales. He said, "We shall see how much food this is worth."

To his astonishment the scale would not go down when he put a loaf of bread on the other side. To his confusion and embarrassment, it would not go down though he kept on adding food, anything he could lay his hands on quickly, because people were watching him.

He tried to be gruff and he was making a bad job of it. His face got red and it made him angry to be flustered. So finally he said, "Well, that's all the scales will hold anyway. Here's a bag. You'll have to put it in yourself. I'm busy."

With what sounded like a gasp or a little sob, she took the bag and started packing in the food, wiping her eyes on her sleeves every time her arm was free to do so. He tried not to look, but he could not help seeing that he had given her a pretty big bag and that it was not quite full. So he tossed a large cheese down the counter, but he did not say anything; nor did he see the timid smile of grateful understanding which glistened in her moist eyes.

When the woman had gone, he went to look at the scales, scratching his head and shaking it in puzzlement. Then he found the solution. The scales were broken.

The grocer never saw the woman again. Yet for the rest of his life he remembered her better than any other woman in the world and thought of her often. He kept the slip of paper the woman handed him. It simply read, "Please, Lord, give us this day our daily bread" (Matt. 6:11).

God does hear your prayers in the night-time and is able to help you even if it takes breaking a scale to do it. His ways are above our ways and beyond our understanding, but He will answer your prayer and help you in the midnight of your life. When the fire is the hottest, He will be the closest. He promised in Jeremiah 33:3 that He would help. "Call unto me, and I will answer thee, and shew thee great and mighty things, which thou knowest not."

You do not have to know everything. You do not even have to understand everything, just leave it in His hands. Do all you can do, and then leave the miracle to Him.

A Chinese convert, when asked by a missionary what remedy he found most effective in curing his fellow-countrymen of the opium habit, idolatry, fear of persecution, and other sins, replied simply, "Knee medicine." Jesus said it so well, "Men ought always to pray and NOT TO FAINT" (Luke 18:1).

Paul gave the secret to victory in 1 Timothy 2:1, "I exhort therefore, that, first of all, supplications, prayers, intercessions, and giving of thanks, be made for all men." The first order of business is prayer. If prayer was made first, a lot of our problems would not exist. Many times we plunge in and do things, and then pray about it. The old saying, "An ounce of prevention is worth a pound of cure," is true. This is also true of prayer, "An ounce of prayer first is worth a pound of cure." Nevertheless, prayer is for all occasions. Prayer is communication with the Deity. Prayers never die, (see Revelation 5:8), and they set things in motion as in the case of Esther and her people.

Esther was the daughter of Abihail who lived at Shushan, the Persian royal city. When her parents died she came under the guardian care of Mordecai, a palace official to whom she was related by marriage. Mordecai had a deep affection for her and reared her as his own daughter. When the time came for King Ahasuerus to choose a queen to serve with him, Esther was one of the maidens from which he was to choose. When Esther walked before the king he loved her above all the women, and she obtained grace and favor in his sight.

As it will happen, nothing is ever perfect, and so it happened in Esther's life. There was a certain man in the kingdom named Haman who was vain, egotistical, and ambitious to the point that he destroyed anyone who got in his way. When Esther's uncle did not bow down to him, it so angered Haman that he plotted to kill Mordecai. When he found out Mordecai was a Jew, he found his plot.

He went to the king and planted a lie in the king's mind concerning the Jews. He said, "There is a certain people scattered abroad and dispersed among the people in all the provinces of thy kingdom; and their laws are diverse from all people; neither keep they the king's laws; therefore it is not for the king's profit to suffer them. If it please the king, let it be written that they may be destroyed" (Esther 3:8-9).

What he did not know was that Esther was also a Jew. When the king gave Haman permission to have them destroyed and news reached the doomed people, what did they do? "And in every province, whithersoever the king's commandment and his decree came, there was great mourning among the Jews, and fasting, and weeping, and wailing; and many lay in sackcloth and ashes" (Esther 4:3).

The fervent prayers started in the ash pile, but they did not stay there. They ascended straight to the throne of God and He heard them. What was the next order of business? Well, Queen Esther heard about the decree and she was grieved also, so what did she do? She prayed and fasted three days with her maidens and then made the decision to go before King Ahasuerus even if he had not called her, which could mean certain death. She said, "If I perish, I perish" (Esther 4:16).

After having gone before the king and gaining his favor, she asked him to come to a banquet she had prepared, and to bring Haman also. This pleased the king and he granted it unto her. After the first banquet Esther invited them both for a second one, and they both agreed to come. This banquet was Haman's downfall.

Esther revealed the plot that Haman had made against her and her people, and it angered the king so much that he arose from the table and walked into the garden. When the king walked back into the room he saw Haman on the queen's bed, begging her to forgive him. This added fuel to the fire and the king said, "Will he force the queen also before me in the house?" (Esther 7:8).

The very gallows that Haman had made for the destruction of Mordecai were used for his destruction. "So they hanged Haman on the gallows that he had prepared for Mordecai. Then was the king's wrath pacified" (Esther 7:10). Revenge always backfires!

The destroying factor in Esther's life had been destroyed. How? It all started with strong cries, fervent prayers, and calling to God down in the ashes. While you are on the ash heap of life you can either build a shrine that will destroy you, or you can build a shrine of prayer and worship to the true God who will deliver you. Hot prayers always touch the heart of God.

God promised, "Then shall ye call upon me, and ye shall go and pray unto me, and I will hearken unto you. And ye shall seek me, and find me, when ye shall search for me with all your heart. And I will be found of you, saith the Lord" (Jer. 29:12-14).

"He will regard the prayer of the destitute, and not despise their prayer" (Ps. 102:17).

Learn from the Camel

The camel, at the close of the day,
Kneels down upon the sandy plain
To have his burden lifted off
And rest again.
My soul, thou too shouldst fall to thy knees
When daylight draweth to a close,
And let thy Master lift the load
And give repose.
The camel kneels at morning's dawn
To have the guide replace his load —
Then rises up anew, to take
The desert road . . . .
— Wheaton Anthology[4]

16

MIND ON FIRE

There are several things that must be done so the gods or shrines from the ashes can be replaced by an allegiance to the real God. One thing that you can do is found in 2 Corinthians 10:5. "Casting down imaginations, and every high thing that exalteth itself against the knowledge of God, and bringing into captivity every thought to the obedience of Christ."

A. Cast down imaginations, and every high thing that exalteth itself against the knowledge of God.
B. Bring into captivity every thought to the obedience of Christ.

You have to rise from the ashes and declare war on the enemy who caused the burning. When Jesus got rid of the devil, His enemy, in Matthew 4, He used the Word. Notice the three times the devil came to him with a temptation, He said the first time: "IT IS WRITTEN." The second time He said: "IT IS WRITTEN AGAIN." The third time He said: "Get thee hence,

Satan, FOR IT IS WRITTEN."

When the enemy saw that he could not get Jesus to doubt, hesitate, or give in, verse 11 says, "Then the devil leaveth him."

The Word is the most powerful weapon you can use against your thoughts that are not in conjunction with the will of God. The part of the armor used to fight off the enemy in hand-to-hand combat is the sword. Ephesians 6:17 says that the sword is the Word of God. You need to slice and cut away the shrines that have taken a dominate place in your mind.

Hebrews 4:12 says, "For the word of God is quick, and powerful, and sharper than any two-edged sword, piercing even to the dividing asunder of soul and spirit, and of the joints and marrow, and is a discerner of the thoughts and intents of the heart."

Notice how closely knit 2 Corinthians 10:5 and Hebrews 4:12 are. They both talk about thoughts. The Word will reveal to you the condition of your thoughts, heart, and spirit. It not only will reveal to you the wrong strongholds and the idols that are set up in your heart and thoughts, but it will help bring them down, clean them out, and to establish the right strongholds. The Word will develop new captains of faith, hope, courage, love, forgiveness, and mercy. The Word is that powerful.

After you clean out the thoughts and replace the strongholds, there is maintenance involved. Anything that is left alone is going to crumble. I heard of a brand new house that was built out on the edge of town and left alone for ten years. At the end of ten years when they opened the door, they found that the spiders, rodents, and weather had taken their toll. The house was filled with spider's webs, cracks, and partial collapse in some areas, simply because of total neglect.

There has to be maintenance. Peter said, "Wherefore gird up the loins of your mind, be sober and hope to the end" (1 Pet. 1:13). There must be a tightening of the part of the mind that is able to reproduce. Genesis 35:11 shows that the loins have generative power. "And God said unto him, I am God Almighty: be fruitful and multiply; a nation and a company of nations shall be of thee, and kings shall come out of thy loins."

The loins of the mind produce many thoughts. One writer said, "No man is wise enough by himself." Your mind needs to be rejuvenated, inspired, and cleaned out by something outside itself. Philippians 4:8 instructs us on what to dwell on. "Finally, brethren, whatsoever things are true, whatsoever things are honest, whatsoever things are just, whatsoever things are pure, whatsoever things are lovely, whatsoever things are of good report; if there be any virtue, and if there be any praise, think on these things." You cannot treat your mind disrespectfully and expect it to respect you. Your mind is a gift from God and if you abuse it, it will abuse you. You are the captain over all the captains of the strongholds that are allowed to dwell in your mind. You have the power and authority to disengage any thought that is hurting you. The Word of God would not have given instruction to do so if you did not have the power to do so.

There was once an old lion who was too weak to hunt or fight for his food, who decided that he must get it by his wits. He lay down in a cave, pretending to be ill, and whenever any animals came to visit him, he seized them and ate them. After many had perished in this way, a fox who had seen through the trick came and stood at a distance from the cave, and inquired how he was. "Bad," the lion answered, and asked why he did not come in.

"I would have come in," said the fox, "but I saw a lot of tracks going in and none coming out."

The moral of the story is that the enemy of your soul entices you to come in and visit with him and his thoughts. He will lie to you for he is the father of lies, and he will seize you and force you to die spiritually by his cunning. The thing to do is stay out of his cave and live. Let the Word of God be your wisdom to know which cave to go into and which one not to enter. Wise up to the wiles of the devil and when you do encounter troubles and sorrows caused by other people, do not let it kill you.

Instead of holding counsel with the destroyer and dwelling on the hurts, replace the well-worn tape with a fresh one from the Word of God. It never fails to inspire, uplift, and give hope.

His Word is the thing that brings you health. "Why art thou cast down, O my soul? and why art thou disquieted within me? hope thou in God: for I shall yet praise him, who is the health of my countenance, and my God" (Ps. 42:11).

If you need a cure for a mind that is disturbed, disquieted, and in turmoil, Joshua gives the formula for living successfully by not allowing the turbulence of life to affect you. "This book of the law shall not depart out of thy mouth; but thou shalt meditate therein day and night, that thou mayest observe to do according to all that is written therein: for then thou shalt make thy way prosperous, and then thou shalt have good success" (Josh. 1:8).

Your mind needs to get on fire with the promises of God's Word, so the dross of Satan's lies and men's carnal wisdom can be burned out of it. When your mind is stayed on God, you are guaranteed peace.

"Thou wilt keep him in perfect peace, whose MIND is stayed on thee: because he trusteth in thee" (Isa. 26:3).

In Alberta, where they experience very cold weather, there is one spot in the province where in spite of the frigid weather the grass is always green. In 1919 an underground fire in the coal mine of Cadomin broke out. The fire has never been extinguished, and to this day it continues to burn. In the coldest days of winter the grass above the fire remains summer green.

Does that not remind you of the passage of Scripture in Jeremiah 17:5-8? "Thus saith the Lord; Cursed be the man that trusteth in man, and maketh flesh his arm, and whose heart departeth from the Lord. For he shall be like the heath in the desert, and shall not see when good cometh; but shall inhabit the parched places in the wilderness, in a salt land and not inhabited. Blessed is the man that trusteth in the Lord, and whose hope the Lord is. For he shall be as a tree planted by the waters, and that spreadeth out her roots by the river, and shall not see when heat cometh, but her LEAF SHALL BE GREEN; and shall not be careful in the year of drought, neither shall cease from yielding fruit."

God can give you victory in the trial if you trust in Him, and learn to travel through life without getting bogged down with too many things. You are born into the world naked, and then the accumulation starts. Clothes, toys, and equipment enough for a small army are gathered, for just one tiny baby. This is just the beginning. The older you get, the more things you will purchase and hoard. Just as you accumulate things that can be seen, you also adopt attitudes and spirits. Your mind becomes a trunk that stores both good and bad experiences from the past. The load in your mind can cause you to have a short circuit.

Alexander the Great was marching on Persia, and it looked as if the great empire was about to crumble, as later it did. There was a critical moment, however, which nearly resulted in disaster. The army had taken spoils of silver, gold, and other treasures in such quantities that the soldiers were literally weighed down with them. Alexander gathered all the spoils together in one great pile and set fire to them.

The soldiers were furious, but it was not long before they realized the wisdom of their leader. It was as if wings had been given to them — they walked lightly again. They were victorious that day over the enemy, but first they had to get rid of some things.

Jesus warned about getting bogged down with the cares of life. He said, "And take heed to yourselves, lest at any time your hearts be overcharged with surfeiting, and drunkenness, and cares of this life . . . Watch ye therefore, and pray always" (Luke 21:34,36).

What good are things if they hamper our walk in life? What good are debilitating thoughts if they keep us from victory? It is time to set a bonfire in your mind and throw every thought, attitude, and spirit that exalts itself above the knowledge of God, into the fire and burn them. Then as the soldiers walked, you will walk once again with a spring in your step, light and lively. The birds will sing and you will hear them. The sun will shine and you will feel it. The trees will gently make music by the rustling of their leaves and it will set music in motion in your heart. You will be free from the fetters, cares of life, and chains that seem to hold you every time you move.

17

PRAISE IN THE FIRE

When the enemy's fire comes to you, just turn around and burn him by burning sweet incense to God. Job burnt Satan by worshipping. When he lost everything and it looked like he was consumed by the enemy's fire, he sinned not with his lips. "Then Job arose, and rent his mantle, and shaved his head, and fell down upon the ground; AND WORSHIPPED" (Job 1:20).

Fire was a part of the Old Testament rituals and offering of sacrifice. Moses was commanded by God to burn sweet incense unto God. "And he burnt sweet incense thereon; as the Lord commanded Moses" (Exod. 40:27).

Hebrews 13:10 says, "We have an altar." Jesus became our sacrifice. "By him, therefore let us offer the sacrifice of praise to God, continually, that is, the fruit of our lips giving thanks to his name" (Heb. 13:15-16).

Praise Him not only in your mind, but also aloud. Over and over the Psalms instruct us to lift up our

voice in praise. The act of praise eliminates Satan's lies and destroying power. Praise has a positive affect on the body, mind, and spirit. There is something uplifting to praising verbally with our lips as instructed to do in Hebrews.

> I will bless the Lord at all times: his praise shall continually be in my **mouth** (Ps. 34:1).
>
> And he hath put a new song in my **mouth**, even praise unto our God; many shall see it, and fear, and shall trust in the Lord (Ps. 40:3).
>
> O clap your hands, all ye people; shout unto God with the **voice of triumph** (Ps. 47:1).
>
> Sing aloud unto God our strength: make a joyful **noise** unto the God of Jacob (Ps. 81:1).
>
> Then was our **mouth** filled with laughter, and our **tongue** with singing: then said they among the heathen, The Lord hath done great things for them (Ps. 126:2).
>
> Let every thing that hath breath praise the Lord (Ps. 150:6).

Jesus, who knew the power of the spoken word, said in Mark 11:23, "For verily I say unto you, That whosoever shall **say** unto this mountain, Be thou removed, and be thou cast into the sea; and shall not doubt in his heart, but shall believe that those things which he **saith** shall come to pass; he shall have whatsoever he **saith**." The spoken word is powerful.

Science tells us that words which are spoken never die, but are continually in the atmosphere. It has been reported that scientists are working on a machine that will recapture voices from the past. Who knows what they will be able to do? Many years ago no one believed a man could walk on the moon.

If our words are forever floating around in the atmosphere, why not let them be words of praise, power, and faith? You can create a lifestyle of giving praise. Just as grumbling becomes a habit, so can praise become a habit. Anything as powerful as praise needs to be developed into our lives as an integral part. Praise works! A friend of mine, Elizabeth Cripps, and I were working on mail-outs when she shared a vision with me that she had one night several years ago. As she was telling it her voice throbbed with emotion and tears ran down her cheeks as she recalled so vividly the details as if it were yesterday. In her darkness Christ gave her beauty for ashes. These were her words:

> During a particularly difficult time in our lives, my husband and I were on a fast. He was up into the wee hours of the morning praying for me that I might be encouraged. About 3:00 a.m. I was awakened with this vision:
>
> I was looking down from the sky upon a dark and dismal road that a lady was fearfully walking down. The lady was me, and life was dark, uncertain, and very threatening. I could not see anything surrounding me, only the path winding downward before me. All of a sudden the thought came to me that I had nothing to lose and I threw my hands in the air and began to praise and worship God. Then from across the sky I saw a very angry animal-like face appear, and in

its fury it sent bolts of lightning to destroy me. Just as the bolts were about to strike me, a large hand, which I knew to be God's, came in front of me with a shield so shiny that when the lightening struck it, the whole sky lit up and there was such beauty around me and rainbow-like colors appeared in the sky. Then I knew the beauty was there all along, it was only the darkness that hid it from my view. What the enemy had intended for evil, the Lord intended for my good.

When the angel appeared unto Abram in a vision he said, "Fear not, Abram, I AM THY SHIELD, and thy exceeding great reward" (Gen. 15:1). Just as God became Abram's shield, He also became Elizabeth Cripp's shield. He is also your shield, but notice what brought the shield around her. It was praise and worship to God.

I heard a tape that had been recorded three or four generations ago. It was the story of seven people who had gone into a little church and begun to praise and worship God, singing the song "Hallelujah." There was an old man who recorded this. When he played it back, to their great surprise, there were many voices on the tape. They were not human voices, but the voices of angels.

When a scientist listened to the phenomenon he said that in the scientific world they are aware that at all times there are voices in the atmosphere continually giving praise to God. The voices I listened to were singing high praises majestically and never taking a breath as humans need to do. It was a breathtaking experience listening to the throb of worship unto the King of kings.

Praise is where the victory is. When Paul and Silas were beaten and thrown into prison they prayed and sang praises at midnight, and God caused an earthquake to come and the prison doors opened and they were set free. (See Acts 16:25.) The praise at midnight opened the doors and the bands fell off.

You will pass through your midnights. There will be pain, fiery trials, and disappointments, but praise will cause the constricting bands of fear and disillusionment to fall off you. Prayer and praise opens doors of prisons quicker than anything else. It is God's way to bring you victory.

Men and women of the Bible who went through great trials intrigue me. There is one characteristic they all have in common: praying, praising, worshipping, or thanking God in the time of their greatest trouble or trial. Some of them were:

Daniel — When he knew he was going to be thrown in the lion's den, he prayed and **thanked** his God as he had been doing every day for many years (see Dan. 2:23).

Abraham — On the day of his greatest sacrifice, with a bleeding heart, when he and his son were going to obey the Lord and someone asked him where he was going, he replied, "I and the lad will go and **worship**" (see Gen. 22:5).

Anna — A widow who could have developed into a recluse in bitterness and loneliness gave herself to daily **prayers** and fastings unto the Lord (see Luke 2:37).

Hannah — The day of her greatest sacrifice; leaving her young son at the temple of the Lord, she prayed and said, "My heart rejoiceth in the Lord." She continued to worship the great God that had given her a child in her barrenness (see 1 Samuel. 2:1).

Paul — Shortly before his martyrdom he wrote many things that give insight to his inner thinking. Instead of being bitter and blaming God for his days of imprisonment, he wrote encouraging letters that show his attitude and prayer life. He wrote: "I thank God, whom I serve from my forefathers with pure conscience, that without ceasing I have remembrance of thee in my **prayers** day and night" (2 Tim. 1:3). "For God hath not given us the spirit of fear; but of power, and of love, and of a sound mind" (2 Tim. 1:7).

Everyone, sooner or later, will experience heartaches, hurts, and disappointments. Joseph was lied about, rejected, and mocked, yet he kept his integrity with God and continued to pray daily until God brought him out victorious. Your attitude during the time of being burnt determines your destiny. Joseph was burnt to the fullest degree, but it did not make him bitter. Whatever you encounter in life, learn to pray and praise like those before us and be victorious as they were.

Life has not always been roses for myself and my family. We have shared many heartaches as well as the joys of life. There are times when we reflect back over our lives, and it seems the times when we had the most victory during our trials was when we prayed and praised.

When mother passed away I was a young thirty-two-year old. I remember our family with my brothers and sisters standing in the hallway of our home waiting for the funeral car to come and take us to the memorial service at the church. We were standing there singing a praise song to our God. It was the same song that had been recorded on the tape with the seven worshippers in the little country church. We sang simply "Hallelujah, Hallelujah!" Even now I can still see the scene as we stood there with tears running down our cheeks. It seemed that a special presence of the Lord filled the room and carried us through the whole funeral with such peace.

Over and over we have practiced this during the times when our hearts have been broken by circumstances and hurtful relationships. It seems that God has always helped us through the most difficult times when we would praise Him instead of hardening our hearts and complaining about what a raw deal was handed to us. There were times when we did complain, and struggled against bitterness becoming lodged in our hearts. Then we would fall at His feet and He would give us grace to go on and help us to be able to praise Him even when we did not want to at first. Oh, but the joy that comes by doing it His way!

It is not easy to do this when you are bleeding and you want to get even, but it is God's way and it works. He said, "In every thing give thanks; for this is the will of God in Christ Jesus concerning you" (1 Thess. 5:18).

Quote this chapter before you begin your day and then practice it in the good times as well as the bad times.

PSALM 150

1. Praise ye the Lord. Praise God in his sanctuary: praise him in the firmament of his power.

2. Praise him for his mighty acts: praise him according to his excellent greatness.

3. Praise him with the sound of the trumpet: praise him with the psaltery and harp.

4. Praise him with the timbrel and dance: praise him with stringed instruments and organs.

5. Praise him upon the loud cymbals: praise him upon the high sounding cymbals.

6. Let every thing that hath breath praise the Lord. Praise ye the Lord.

Rudyard Kipling, who gained renown throughout the world as a poet and storyteller, made this statement: "We have forty million reasons for failure, but not a single excuse."

You can give all the reasons why you cannot praise during your difficult times, but there is *nothing* that can stop you if you desire to do it.

You will never be the person you can be if pressure, trials, and struggles are taken out of your life, so determine to praise God for the *better* person He is allowing you to become.

Epilogue

There is negative fire (the enemy's) and there is positive fire (God's). When the enemy causes you to be burnt by someone, you will be tempted to build shrines of bitterness, anger, and unforgiveness. Also, when you are privileged to handle and touch God's fire, you will be tempted to let the ashes stack up through pride, prayerlessness, or doubt. They will become banked and hardened, making it difficult to let His fire flow freely and effectively in you.

You must daily do as the priests of the Old Testament did. Get the shovel and clean out the ashes — whether they are ashes that have been built into negative shrines from the enemy's fire or ashes from God's holy fire that have become bigger than the fire, thus making it difficult to let God's Word and Spirit become effective in your life. Build your life on the Rock, Christ Jesus, and the enemy cannot destroy your foundation. You can build again, but as you build always remember to clean out the ashes.

God will ignite a flame inside of you that will inspire all who know you. He gives you the fire of inspiration and excitement! The enemy will try to extinguish and stifle your enthusiasm; for he desires that you live in a blazing inferno of devastation and sorrow. But God has all power and will give you the confidence to live a constructive life of hope and power. God is on your side, and with Him you always win!

Notes

Preface
[1]Dean C. Dutton, Ph.D., arr. & comp., *Quests and Conquests* (Guthrie, OK: Live Service Publishing Co., 1923), p. 9.

Chapter 1
[1]Ibid. p. 8.
[2]Clinton T. Howell, ed., *Lines to Live By* (Nashville, TN: Thomas Nelson Publishers, 1972), p. 177.

Chapter 2
[1]Paul Lee Tan, ThD., *Encyclopedia of 7,700 Illustrations: Signs of the Times* (Rockville, MD: Assurance Publishers, 1979), p. 337.
[2]Joseph S. Johnson, comp., *A Field of Diamonds* (Nashville, TN: Broadman Press, 1974), p. 175.

Chapter 4
[1]Herbert V. Prochnow, *The Public Speaker's Treasure Chest* (New York, NY: Harper & Bros. Publ., 1942), p. 330.
[2]William Shakespeare, *The Tragedy of King Richard II* (Baltimore, MD: Penguin Books, 1970).
[3]Tan, *Encyclopedia of 7,700 Illustrations*, p. 542.
[4]Lillian Eichler Watson, ed. & comm., *Light from Many Lamps* (New York, NY: Simon & Schuster, 1951), p. 205.
[5]Tan, *Encyclopedia of 7,700 Illustrations*, p.1358.

Chapter 5
[1]Corrie Ten Boom, *Corrie Ten Boom — Her Life, Her Faith* (Old Tappan, NJ: F.H. Revell Co., 1983).

Chapter 6
[1]Watson, *Light from Many Lamps*, p. 92.
[2]Ibid, p. 87.
[3]Dale Carnegie, *How to Stop Worrying and Start Living* (New York, NY: Simon and Schuster, 1948), p.153.
[4]Prochnow, *The Public Speaker's Treasure Chest*, p. 321.

Chapter 7
[1]Howell, *Lines to Live By*, p. 133.
[2]*Childcraft, The How and Why Library*, I11, Vol. 12.

Chapter 8

[1]Marie King, *The Gold Star Family Album*, Arthur and Nancy DeMoss, eds. (Old Tappan, NJ: Fleming H. Revell Co., 1968), p. 160.

[2]A. Hamming, *Half-Hour Talks on Character Building by Self-Made Men and Women*, J.S. Kurtley, D.D., ed., 1910, p. 407.

[3]Dutton, *Quests and Conquests*, p. 9.

Chapter 9

[1]Dutton, *Quests and Conquests*, Number 414.

[2]Tan, *Encyclopedia of 7,700 Illustrations*, p. 220.

[3]Howell, *Lines to Live By*, p. 15.

[4]Ibid., p. 16.

Chapter 10

[1]H.A. Ironside, Litt.D., *Illustrations of Bible Truth* (Chicago, IL: Moody Press, 1945), p. 97.

Chapter 11

[1]Watson, *Light from Many Lamps*, p. 66-67.

[2]Tan, *Encyclopedia of 7,700 Illustrations*, p. 1669.

Chapter 12

[1]Hamming, *Half-Hour Talks*, p. 478.

Chapter 13

[1]Howell, *Lines to Live By*, p. 160.

[2]Dr. Herbert Lockyer, R.S.L., *The Women of the Bible* (Grand Rapids, MI: Zondervan Publ. House, 1967).

[3]*Matthew Henry's Commentary on the Whole Bible* (Marshallton, DE: The National Foundation for Christian Education, 1845), Vol. III, N. Test.

[4]Tan, *Encyclopedia of 7,700 Illustrations*, p. 519.

Chapter 14

[1]*Matthew Henry's Commentary*, Vol. IV, Isaiah to Malachi.

[2]Dutton, *Quests and Conquests*, p. 15.

Chapter 15

[1]Watson, *Light from Many Lamps*, p. 67.

[2]Alexander Lake, *Your Prayers Are Always Answered* (New York, NY: Simon & Schuster, 1956), p. 208.

[3]Ibid.

[4]Johnson, *A Field of Diamonds*, p. 146.

DATE DUE

Copyright 1998

PRINTED IN U.S.A.

LIVING WITH SHINGLES

Living with Shingles

New Hope for an Old Disease

Mary-Ellen Siegel

Gray Williams, Jr.

M. Evans and Company, Inc.
New York

M. Evans and Company, Inc.
216 East 49th Street
New York, New York 10017

Library of Congress Cataloging-in-Publication Data

Siegel, Mary-Ellen.
   Living with shingles : new hope for an old disease / Mary-Ellen Siegel and Gray Williams.
      p.   cm.
   Includes bibliographical references and index.
   ISBN 0-87131-828-8 (hardcover)
   1. Shingles (Disease)—Popular works.   I. Williams, Gray, 1932–   .   II. Title.
   RC147.H6S56   1998
   616.5'22—dc21   98-8031

DESIGN AND TYPESETTING BY RIK LAIN SCHELL

Printed in the United States of America

9   8   7   6   5   4   3   2   1

In loving memory of Hermine,
sister, friend, and staunchest ally
M.E.S.

To my daughters, Julie, Meredith, and Dar, Who
light my life
G.W.

Acknowledgments

Thank you to all those who support my professional endeavors: my family as well as my friends and colleagues in the Department of Community and Preventive Medicine (Social Work and Behavioral Sciences) at the Mount Sinai School of Medicine. I am especially grateful to Drs. Helen Rehr, Gary Rosenberg, and Susan Blumenfield.

M.E.S.

Thanks to the many friends and relations who generously shared their own experiences with me, and helped me to gain a more personal perspective concerning this painful medical disorder.

G.W.

We are very appreciative of the efforts of Albert Lefkovits, M.D., Charles Stacy, M.D., Jacqueline Lustgarten, M.D., Brian Blakley, M.D., Ph.D., Richard Perkin, and Liliana Coletti Dacosta for their encouragement and numerous suggestions in the preparation of the manuscript. A special thank you to Mike Cohn, who brought us together on this project and to each other for so much.

M.E.S. and G.W.

CONTENTS

FOREWORD

Until recently, physicians had little to offer patients suffering from a reactivation of the chickenpox virus, the condition called herpes zoster, more commonly known as shingles. In the past, physicians could only offer palliative therapy and home remedies. When anti-viral drugs were introduced, the picture changed, and we began to feel encouraged that truly effective treatment was available.

Today physicians are seeing many more patients with shingles because there has been a growth in the population most vulnerable to developing this viral disease. This includes the aged, patients treated with radiation or chemotherapy for cancer, transplanted organ recipients, people who are HIV positive, and anyone else whose immune system has

LIVING WITH SHINGLES

been weakened by disease or treatment, or even excessive stress.

Physicians can now offer patients with herpes zoster effective therapy with anti-viral agents if the condition is diagnosed early. If the painful condition known as post-herpetic neuralgia develops later, judicious use of carefully selected antidepressives, anti-seizure medications, and palliatives, can be helpful in ameliorating the resulting discomfort of post-herpetic neuralgia.

Anyone who suspects that he or she might have shingles should be examined promptly by a physician, since early diagnosis is crucial for effective therapy. The first seventy-two hours after symptoms appear offer a brief "window of opportunity" during which treatment can dramatically decrease the severity and duration of the disease. If a patient's primary physician is not experienced in treating shingles, there should be a prompt referral to a physician who is. Most family or internal medicine physicians and dermatologists are able to treat shingles effectively.

The authors of *Living with Shingles* have researched their subject very carefully and have provided a great deal of information that should help make patients, their relatives, and their friends able to cope with this common illness. The authors stress that prompt treatment is important, and that treatment is an art as well as a science. They offer

4

hope for the present as well as the future in minimizing and even eradicating this condition once referred to as "the devil's grip."

This book is highly recommended to patients who suffer from herpes and post-herpetic neuralgia, to those at high risk for these disorders, and to anyone interested in the ailments.

Albert Lefkovits, M.D.
Assistant Clinical Professor of Dermatology
Mount Sinai School of Medicine, New York

CHAPTER 1

What Is Shingles?

Mark Singer is an avid gardener who spends much of his free time working in his yard. When he was fifty-five, an itchy reddish rash appeared on the fingers of his left hand. At first he thought that he had once again come into contact with poison ivy. But he was annoyed that the usual remedies he used for poison ivy didn't work, and that the rash persisted longer than usual. Still, the itching wasn't serious enough to make him seek medical help. It was only because he had a regular checkup scheduled two weeks after the rash appeared that he mentioned it to his doctor.

LIVING WITH SHINGLES

The doctor examined the rash closely. "That's not poison ivy," he said. "I'm pretty sure you have shingles. Those little blisters are quite distinctive. A mild attack, fortunately. You're already getting over it."

Susan MacDonald was an active, seventy-six-year-old widow who had always enjoyed good health. One morning she awoke feeling slightly feverish, queasy in her stomach, and sore on the left side of her upper chest and back. Within a few hours a slight blotchy rash began to appear in the sore area. Because she had friends who had suffered from shingles, she knew what the symptoms were. She called her doctor to report her suspicions, and he referred her to a dermatologist.

By the time of her appointment next day, some of the small bumps of her rash had swelled into blisters. "It's shingles, all right," the dermatologist told her. "We could run some tests on fluid from those blisters to make sure, but it really isn't necessary. Seems to be only moderately severe. But we'll start treatment right away."

As Fred Weintraub celebrated his eightieth birthday, he was thankful that he had no serious health problems other than the arthritis in his hands and knees, which anti-inflammatory drugs controlled fairly well. One summer weekend, he noticed an odd, cramping feeling in his left chest, rather like a muscle spasm. Over the next two days, the cramping feel-

8

ing developed into a burning pain, which spread from his chest to his back. By the evening of the fourth day, a broad band of reddish rash covered the area. Next morning he went to his doctor, who tentatively diagnosed his condition as shingles, and sent him to a dermatologist.

The dermatologist quickly confirmed the diagnosis. "I'm afraid you have a fairly severe case," he told Fred. "That broad band suggests more than one nerve is involved. And did you say that this is the fifth day since you first noticed the pain? We'll just have to see if we can bring this quickly under control."

LIVING WITH SHINGLES

An Old Enemy, and an Enemy of the Old

The disease called *shingles* has been recognized since ancient times. Its most obvious symptoms—a blistered rash, accompanied by itching or burning pain—have long been well known. Also well known are several other basic facts: It mainly attacks older people, and the older they are the more severe the attack. It almost always affects just one side of the body, and it is limited to a specific area on that side. The most common of these areas is the middle of the trunk; the second most common is the upper part of the face. Finally, and perhaps most importantly, the pain of shingles varies widely, but it can be agonizingly intense. Moreover, the pain may persist long after the rash has disappeared, a condition known as *post-herpetic neuralgia*.

The name *shingles* is somewhat misleading. The word is singular, not plural, and it has nothing to do with building materials. It is derived from the Latin word *cingulum*, which means "belt," and refers to the typical location of the rash, in a horizontal band around part of the chest or abdomen. Another word for shingles is *zoster*, a Greek word which also means belt.

10

A Disorder of the Nerves

Until the nineteenth century, shingles was considered a very mysterious disease. Why, for example, did the rash occur in only a limited area, and on only one side of the body? And what made it so painful? Fundamental discoveries about the nervous system, and the sensory nerves in particular, helped answer these questions. It was discovered that the nerves that register sensations in the skin are laid out in symmetrical pairs, running from the base of the spine to the base of the skull. Each nerve of the pair extends from the skin to one side of the spinal column, where it connects with the nerves of the central nervous system, carrying sensations to the brain. Each nerve registers sensations from only a single body segment, called a *dermatome* (literally, a "skin slice"), and individual branches of the nerve may register sensations from only a part of the dermatome. That is why the area of shingles is limited: It almost always occurs within a single dermatome, or two or three adjacent ones, and it often occurs in only a part of a dermatome.

It was also discovered that the pain of shingles is *neurogenic*. Ordinarily, skin pain originates in the skin itself: injury or irritation causes the skin cells to

11

release chemical substances, which, in turn, stimulate the nearby ends of pain-sensing nerves. Neurogenic pain, by contrast, is produced by damage or malfunction *within* the nerve cells—the *neurons*—that make up the nerves. Neurogenic pain is characteristic of several conditions that are notorious for the suffering they cause. *Trigeminal neuralgia*, or *tic douloureux*, for example, produces shocking, stabbing pain in the face, resulting from damage or irritation to the trigeminal nerve. *Causalgia* produces burning pain in the area of a nerve-damaging injury, such as a severe wound. *Stump pain*, or *phantom limb pain,* may follow the amputation of an arm or leg. The pain of shingles is similar in nature, and it can be equally agonizing.

Discovering the Cause

The basic cause of shingles was not identified until the early 1900s. Fluid from the blisters of shingles was found to contain particles of a virus—the same *varicella* virus that causes the familiar childhood disease of chickenpox. It has therefore come to be known as the *varicella-zoster virus*, or VZV for short. It was also discovered that VZV produces the nerve damage underlying shingles, and that the virus tends to favor certain nerves: those serving the dermatomes of the trunk and head.

But it took several decades more to establish that shingles isn't caused by a new infection of VZV. Rather, the disease results from the reactivation of the same batch of virus that many years earlier caused chickenpox. After recovery from chickenpox, particles of the virus remain alive but dormant, stored in the *dorsal ganglia* of the sensory nerves. Ganglia (literally, "knots") are enlarged portions of the nerve roots, which are located toward the back of the spinal cord (*dorsal* means "back") near the points where they connect with the central nerves. Usually many years after the chickenpox infection, the virus "wakes up" and starts to reproduce in the nerve cells.

13

LIVING WITH SHINGLES

Nerve cells—neurons—have a very unusual shape, compared with other cells. Extending from the main cell body, which contains the nucleus, is a long, thin tube called an *axon*, which contains only cell fluid, or *cytoplasm*. The cell bodies of the sensory neurons serving the skin are located in the dorsal ganglia, but their axons extend all the way out to the skin. The virus reproduces in the cell nucleus, and particles of it migrate through the cytoplasm of the axon. As they travel, they stimulate the neuron, producing neurogenic sensations of pain and itching. When they reach the skin, they are released from the branching ends (*dendrites*) of the axon, producing the characteristic rash.

But why the long gap between chickenpox and shingles? The answer is the body's immune system. When you catch chickenpox, usually during childhood, your immune system learns to identify the virus and will quickly and effectively attack it whenever it invades again. As a result, once you recover, you will almost certainly never have chickenpox again. And although some virus particles "hide out" in dorsal ganglia, the immune system also prevents them from reproducing out of control. But as you grow older, particularly past the age of fifty or so, your immune system becomes steadily weaker. Eventually it may become incapable of identifying and controlling the virus any longer. The result: rapid viral reproduction, and shingles.

14

Further evidence of the crucial importance of the immune system in holding off shingles comes from a group of relatively young individuals who nonetheless develop the disease. These are the *immunosuppressed*—people who lack the protection of a normal immune system. They may be receiving drugs or radiation for cancer, or taking anti-inflammatory corticosteroids for lupus or arthritis. They may be suffering from blood diseases such as leukemia, lymphoma, or Hodgkin's disease. They may have been infected with HIV, the human immunovirus that causes AIDS. They may be taking drugs to prevent tissue rejection after an organ transplant. All these individuals, if they have ever had chickenpox, are at high risk for developing shingles. Moreover, the attacks are likely to be especially severe, and more likely to result in serious complications.

A Growing Epidemic of the Old

Almost all of us get chickenpox, usually during childhood. But only a minority later develop shingles—no one knows why. Nonetheless, shingles is not uncommon. It affects about 600,000 Americans each year, and between ten and twenty percent of the population will have it at some point in their lives. The chances of an attack begin to rise sharply after age fifty. If you haven't had shingles by the time you are eighty, your chances of developing it are about one in two.

Shingles is a growing epidemic of the old. As more of us live longer, more of us will have shingles. Not only will our immune systems become progressively weaker through natural aging, but we will also be more likely to suffer from *other* health problems that harm the immune system. For example, we are more likely to develop, and to be treated for, cancer; chemotherapy and radiation are frequent triggers for shingles. Furthermore, the older we are when we come down with shingles, the more severe the attack is likely to be, and the more likely that it will lead to painful complications like post-herpetic neuralgia.

16

The Course of Shingles

For most people, shingles follows a typical course that lasts from three to five weeks in all. The course tends to be longer if the affected dermatome is on the trunk, less if it is on the face.

Sometimes the attack is triggered by a specific event. Your immune system might have been weakened by some other ailment, or by some drug you have taken. You might have experienced unusual physical stress, ranging from heavy exertion to extreme heat or cold. Or you might have faced serious emotional stress, from anxiety or grief, say, or a major life change. In many cases, however, the attack occurs without warning—"out of the blue."

The earliest symptoms, as the virus begins to reawaken and reproduce, may be so vague and unspecific as to be unrecognizable. You might have mild chills, a low fever, a dull headache, unusual fatigue, or a general feeling of being unwell (*malaise*). As the virus particles begin to travel down the neurons from the dorsal ganglion to the skin, you might experience sensations such as tingling, itching, or "creeping" of the skin in the affected area.

Even if you begin to experience the localized burning or stabbing pain typical of shingles, you still

17

might not recognize it for what it is. The pain of early shingles has been mistaken for many other conditions, such as muscle strain, gallstones, appendicitis, or even a heart attack. But in two or three days, once the virus has reached the skin, the appearance of the distinctive rash should leave little or no doubt about the cause. Only very rarely does shingles occur without this rash.

The rash begins with reddish patches of small bumps called *papules*. These soon turn into blisters called *vesicles*, which are filled with clear lymph fluid. The vesicles enlarge into *pustules*—blisters filled with cloudy pus, which is a mixture of lymph fluid, white blood cells, and dead cell fragments. The pustules break open, and then crust over and dry to scabs. The process takes place in successive, overlapping waves, and usually lasts a week to ten days in all. The scabs may persist two weeks or more before they drop off.

Itching or pain may last until the skin heals, or even beyond. If it continues past five weeks, however, it is defined as post-herpetic neuralgia rather than shingles. That is, it is considered to be caused by lasting physical damage to the nerves rather than by irritation from an active virus.

Curiously enough, although the affected area may register powerful pain sensations, other sensations, such as touch or warmth, may be reduced. While the virus attack makes the pain-sensing nerves more sensitive, it tends to diminish the activity of other sensory nerves. It apparently also diminishes the activity of certain nerve cells that *inhibit* the transmission of pain sensations to the central nervous system. This reduction of inhibition is believed to account, at least in part, for the intensity of neurogenic pain in general, and shingles pain in particular.

You might also experience muscle weakness, or even paralysis, in the affected area. Sometimes the reactivated virus spreads from the dorsal roots of the sensory nerves to the *ventral* (front) roots of the *motor* nerves, which control motion. Usually any such weakness or paralysis disappears when the virus attack subsides.

For most people, shingles is a temporary, self-limiting disorder. It may be very unpleasant, but usually it lasts no more than five weeks, never returns, and has no lasting consequences. But for a minority, the effects may linger. The most common and probably the most distressing of such possible complications is the continuing pain of post-herpetic neuralgia. Also, the surface of the affected skin may be permanently damaged, scarred, and partly numbed. Shingles of the upper face may infect the eye, risking loss of vision. In rare instances, the virus may spread to other parts of the body. In the lungs, it can cause dangerous pneumonia; in the brain, life-threatening meningitis.

What You Will Find in the Rest of This Book

The following chapters of this book will provide you with further useful information about shingles and its complications, and about what can be done about them.

- **Chapter 2. The Varicella-Zoster Virus.** Knowing more about the virus that causes chickenpox and shingles helps us understand the workings of these diseases and the ways that they are treated.

- **Chapter 3. How Shingles Is Treated.** Shingles can't be cured, but it can be controlled, through drugs, physical therapy, and psychological methods—often in combination.

- **Chapter 4. Post-Herpetic Neuralgia.** The pain of shingles can continue long after the rash has healed, and special methods of treatment may be needed to deal with it.

- **Chapter 5. Other Complications of Shingles.** The virus can seriously damage vision or cause devastating infections in other organs, especially if it isn't treated promptly.

- **Chapter 6. Can Shingles Be Prevented? The Varicella Vaccine.** A new vaccine shows promise in preventing chickenpox, and, perhaps, shingles as well.

CHAPTER 2

The Varicella-Zoster Virus

Susan MacDonald wondered how she had gotten shingles. "Is it true," she asked her dermatologist, "that shingles is caused by the same virus as chickenpox?"

"Quite true," replied the doctor.

"Well, my little grandson comes over a lot, and he just had chickenpox," Susan said. "Could I have caught shingles from him?"

"No, the virus is your own," replied the doctor, "left over from the chickenpox you had when you were a child.

"Can I infect anyone else?"

LIVING WITH SHINGLES

"You can't give anybody shingles," the doctor answered. *"But you might be able to give someone chickenpox, if that person hadn't already had it."*

Susan was puzzled. *"I'm not sure I understand,"* she said.

What Is a Virus?

Chickenpox and shingles are both caused by the varicella-zoster virus—*varicella* means chickenpox, and *zoster* means shingles. For simplicity, the name is shortened to VZV. Like all viruses, VZV is very small—thousands of virus particles, or *virions*, would fit into a typical human cell. And it is so simple in structure that it can barely be described as alive.

Each particle of a virus has just two basic parts. The core is composed of a single piece of either DNA or RNA, the long, chainlike molecules that carry the genetic code for reproduction. In VZV, the core is DNA, coiled up like thread on a spool. The other part of the virus is a coating of protein that surrounds and protects the core.

Although viruses are made up of the same materials as complete cells, they lack many essential cell components. They cannot reproduce on their own. Instead, they must invade cells and take over their genetic machinery, turning them into factories for more virus. The generated particles may then migrate from the host cell to invade other cells, spreading the infection.

Viruses are virtually everywhere around us, and we are exposed to them constantly. They can enter our bodies through the smallest cuts or other breaks in our skin, or through the mucous membranes that line many of our organs. Many of them are harmless to us: they can reproduce only in plants or other animals. But many can cause human diseases, ranging from passing indispositions such as the common cold to dreadful scourges such as smallpox, polio, rabies, and yellow fever.

The Herpesviruses

VZV belongs to a family called the *herpesviruses*. Five of these are particularly important in causing human disease. In addition to VZV, they are:

- *Herpes simplex, type 1*, which causes oral herpes, or cold sores.

- *Herpes simplex, type 2*, which causes genital herpes.

- *Epstein-Barr virus*, which causes mononucleosis.

- *Cytomegalovirus*, which causes a very common but often unrecognized disease of the same name, with usually mild, flu-like symptoms.

The herpesviruses share several significant traits, including the following:

- All of them require a human host. They can only reproduce in human cells.

27

- They are all very infectious. They are easily passed on from one human host to another.

- Once they invade a host, they never completely die out. They may become inactive, but they survive as long as the host does.

- Their effects upon the host are controlled by the host's immune system.

The Immune System

The immune system is the body's main defense against outside invaders of all kinds. One of its main functions is to attack potentially harmful microorganisms—bacteria, funguses, and viruses—that make their way into the body. But it has others as well. In many individuals, for instance, the immune system triggers allergic reactions to certain substances they eat, breathe, or touch. The immune system also reacts against any foreign tissue introduced into the body, such as a transplanted organ, and it must be disarmed to keep a transplant from being rejected. And sometimes the immune system behaves abnormally, treating the body's *own* tissues as "foreign," and causing an *autoimmune* disease such as rheumatoid arthritis, multiple sclerosis, or lupus.

The immune system is based upon various kinds of white blood cells and chemical compounds they produce. The system is complex and carefully balanced, involving several different kinds of cells and several different processes. But it has two basic mechanisms. First, it attacks any substances that have been identified as foreign, and it either destroys them or makes them inactive. Second, it learns to recognize

29

many specific foreign substances the first time they enter the body, and then remembers those substances so they can be attacked even faster and more effectively if they ever appear again.

Your Immune System and VZV

Here's how your immune system interacts with VZV. The process is likely to start at some time during childhood, when someone who has chickenpox passes the virus on to you for the first time. Most often, the tiny particles of the virus are transmitted in invisible droplets of exhaled water vapor, which you unknowingly breathe in. The virus invades the mucus membranes of your nose and throat, multiplies quietly but rapidly, and spreads throughout your body. After two or three weeks of incubation, it produces its most conspicuous symptom, a reddish, itchy rash covering much of your skin.

Since this the first invasion by the virus, your immune system doesn't recognize it, and is relatively slow in mounting a counterattack against it. So you must endure a few days of chickenpox while the immune system gains the upper hand. Your rash progresses from bumps to blisters, which break open and eventually scab over and heal.

Throughout this period, you are very contagious, expelling virus in your breath and shedding it in the fluid from your blisters. Any member of your household who hasn't already had chickenpox is extremely likely to catch it. That's why most people get the disease while they are still children.

31

LIVING WITH SHINGLES

By the time you recover, your immune system has not only killed off most of the virus, but has also learned to identify it for future reference. Whenever you are exposed to the virus again (and you probably will be, repeatedly), your immune system will attack it immediately and massively, preventing it from multiplying enough to cause any symptoms. You are now permanently immune to chickenpox.

Like other herpesviruses, the VZV in your body isn't completely dead. As explained in Chapter 1, it retreats and hides out in the roots, or *ganglia*, of your sensory nerves, next to your spinal column. As long as your immune system remains strong and retains its "immune memory," the virus will remain there, contained and harmless.

But at some point your immune system may become weakened by disease or medication. Or, over time, your immune memory for the virus may wane. The triggering circumstances aren't completely understood, but the virus may suddenly begin to reproduce in one or more of the sensory nerves, and then migrate back to the skin. You now have shingles.

Unlike chickenpox, the rash of shingles is localized within the area served by the affected nerve or nerves. The fluid in the rash blisters contains particles of virus, which are infectious. Thus, you can give chickenpox to someone who hasn't already had chickenpox and isn't immune to it. But you can't give shingles directly to anyone.

32

The Varicella-Zoster Virus

Shingles is not only more localized than chicken-pox, but may also be more severe. The nerve irritation is likely to produce not just annoying itching, but burning pain. The acute attack will also persist longer than chickenpox—weeks rather than days.

Unless your immune system is extremely weak, it will eventually regain control over the virus. Indeed, the acute attack should strengthen your immunity to the virus so that you are unlikely to get shingles ever again. Meanwhile, though, the virus may have caused serious damage to the affected sensory nerves. This damage is believed to be the chief cause of the persistent pain called post-herpetic neuralgia. It may last for weeks, months, or even years before finally subsiding.

VZV acts somewhat differently from the other herpesviruses. Whatever survives of the Epstein-Barr virus and cytomegalovirus after the first infection is kept permanently under control by the immune system, and never again produces disease symptoms. By contrast, the cold sores caused by herpes simplex type one and the genital herpes caused by type two are notoriously recurrent. But because the immune system has learned to recognize the viruses and mobilize against them, later attacks are usually less severe than the first one.

Antibodies (Immunoglobulins)

Among the tools the immune system uses to fight infectious invaders are *antibodies,* also known as *immunoglobulins.* These are protein molecules that are produced by certain white blood cells to match specific invaders, such as a particular kind of virus. Whenever an antibody encounters the matching virus, it becomes attached to the virus particle, marking it for destruction by other immune-system cells.

Varicella-zoster immune globulin (VZIG), a concentrate of antibodies to VZV, can be injected into individuals who have recently been exposed to chickenpox and need extra protection against the virus. These include those whose immune systems have been severely weakened by disease or medications. Also included are pregnant women, since chickenpox caught during certain stages of pregnancy can cause birth defects. VZIG can prevent or at least minimize the symptoms of chickenpox so that it is less likely to lead to harmful complications.

One might expect that VZIG might also be helpful in controlling attacks of shingles and preventing post-herpetic neuralgia. Alas, this treatment has been tried without success. Adding extra antibodies doesn't give the immune system enough strength to keep the virus from proliferating in the neurons. The only effective way to cut down virus reproduction is with *antiviral* drugs, which will be discussed in the next chapter.

Vaccines

The reason that diseases like smallpox, polio, and rabies are no longer such frightening threats to humanity is that effective vaccines have been developed against them.

The first and still the most famous of these is the smallpox vaccine, which provided a model for the others. Through the ages, periodic smallpox epidemics killed or disfigured multitudes of people. In the eighteenth century, a physician named Edward Jenner noticed that people who caught a mild rash disease from handling infected cows never came down with smallpox. He collected fluid from the blisters of this cowpox and pricked it into the skin of people who had never had smallpox. They, too, proved to be permanently immune to smallpox. The serum he used was called a *vaccine* (from a Latin word for *cow*), and the process was named vaccination. Eventually, as we know, vaccination wiped out smallpox.

Jenner didn't know why the vaccine worked—only that it did. Cowpox and smallpox are, in fact, both caused by viruses, and the viruses are very similar. When the vaccine containing cowpox virus enters the body, the immune system learns to recognize the virus and to fight off any future infections

36

of it. But the immune system also reacts the same way toward the smallpox virus, giving immunity to that disease as well.

The vaccines developed since then have been based upon the specific viruses themselves. The virus is either killed or seriously weakened (*attenuated*) so that it cannot multiply and cause disease. But when the vaccine containing it is introduced into the body, enough of its chemical structure remains for the immune system to identify it and form antibodies against it. The result is immunity to the disease, either temporary or permanent.

In recent years, a vaccine for VZV has been developed, and it is now approved for use in the United States. VZV will be discussed in more detail in the last chapter of this book. Suffice it to say here that the vaccine is highly effective in preventing chickenpox, and it may prove to be effective against shingles as well.

CHAPTER 3

How Shingles Is Treated

Mark Singer's doctor was reassuring. "You're lucky," he said. "You're relatively young, your symptoms are mild, and your rash is already partly healed."

"Is there anything I should do about it at this stage?" Mark asked.

"Not unless the itching bothers you. You can use many of the same salves and lotions as you do for poison ivy."

"That's all?" Mark asked.

"That's all. There's no use in fighting the virus at this point. The rash will soon heal by itself, and you shouldn't have any more trouble."

LIVING WITH SHINGLES

Susan MacDonald's dermatologist was optimistic. "It's good you came in so promptly," she said. "The earlier we catch shingles, the better. We'll start you off right away with an antiviral."

"What does that do?" asked Susan.

"It's the one drug we can offer you," the doctor replied, "that will actually attack the virus. Stops it from reproducing in your nerves. It won't immediately stop the rash and discomfort, but you'll hurt less, and, more important, you should recover faster."

"I won't be taking antibiotics?"

"We're often asked that question," the doctor said. "Antibiotics are for bacterial infections. They don't affect viruses at all. I'd only prescribe an antibiotic if there was some sign of a secondary bacterial infection."

"Meanwhile, what can I do for these stabbing pains, and the itching?" Susan asked.

"A variety of things. But you may have to experiment. Different things work better for different people. And again I have to warn you. Nothing is going to give you one hundred percent relief until you're finally healed. In your case, though, I feel sure we can keep you fairly comfortable."

How Shingles Is Treated

Fred Weintraub's dermatologist was frank. "You first felt changes in your skin five days ago, and the rash didn't appear until yesterday. That delay, along with your age and your serious symptoms, means that treatment may not work as well as we'd like. We'll start by attacking the virus infection and making you as comfortable as possible. And then we'll have to see what should be done next. It's hard to predict."

The Arsenal against Shingles

Before so much was known about the cause and course of shingles, a lot of different treatments were tried to relieve it—most of them ineffective. Even now, no treatment provides a quick, complete cure. But modern medical science offers a range of drugs and other treatments that today are of demonstrated helpfulness.

These treatments fall into two main classes:

- *Antiviral drugs,* which attack the virus that causes the disease, relieving the symptoms and hastening recovery.

- *Palliative remedies,* which relieve the symptoms of the disease even if they don't affect its course. These include pain-relieving drugs, taken internally or applied topically, and techniques to reduce the psychological stress that often intensifies pain.

How Shingles Is Treated

Treating the pain of shingles, like treating other forms of pain, is often best accomplished by using a combination of approaches: antiviral drugs, internal painkillers, topical medications, and techniques for managing stress.

Antiviral Drugs

The antiviral drugs used to treat shingles all work in much the same way. They do not kill the virus the way that antibiotics kill bacteria. But they do stop it from reproducing, thus limiting its power to do harm. Moreover, the drugs act selectively upon the virus and have little or no effect on normal cells.

The process has three successive steps. First, when an antiviral drug is absorbed into an infected nerve cell, it provokes the virus there to produce an *enzyme*—a protein molecule that promotes a specific chemical reaction in other molecules. The second step is the reaction the enzyme promotes: the conversion of the drug molecule into a molecule that is similar to one of the building blocks of the viral DNA. Finally, as the virus tries to copy its DNA to form the cores of new particles, a converted drug molecule is substituted into each partial copy so that the formation of the copy cannot be completed. In short, the parent virus can't have offspring—it isn't killed, but it can no longer reproduce.

That's why early treatment of shingles is so important. Antiviral drugs don't destroy the virus that has already invaded the nerve cells, nor can they repair any damage that has already been done. They can only prevent the virus from proliferating and causing even more damage. Thus, they can shorten the course of shingles and make its symptoms milder, but they cannot provide a quick or complete cure. The more time the virus remains active before being checked, the less help the drugs can provide. Indeed, after three days or so, they are likely to be ineffective. So dosage should begin just as soon as a diagnosis of shingles can be made.

Unfortunately, that is easier said than done. The early symptoms of shingles are notoriously vague and unspecific, and are easily mistaken for something else. The only sure sign of shingles is its rash. And although the rash usually appears just a day or two after the tingling or pain, it may be delayed for several days, or even weeks. But you should go on "shingles alert" and seek the advice of your doctor if you experience the following:

- The tingling, itching, or pain occurs in a single area of your body.

- The sensation occurs on just one side of the midline, even though it may extend from the front around to the back.

- It grows progressively stronger and more constant.

LIVING WITH SHINGLES

- The pain feels sharp, stabbing, or burning (rather than, say, a dull ache).

- It seems to diminish somewhat when you lie down and relax.

And, of course, if you see any signs of a rash—even a few scattered bumps—in the affected area, you should get in touch with your doctor immediately.

Antiviral drugs are now recommended for virtually anyone who has shingles, even though the attack may be relatively mild. Three of these drugs are the most widely used for treating shingles. The oldest is acyclovir, which has been in use for several years. Originally it was administered only by intravenous injection, and it is still employed that way in very serious cases. But now it is usually taken by mouth. The trade name for the pill form is Zovirax.

Zovirax isn't absorbed very efficiently from the digestive tract, so it requires five doses a day, taken every four hours except at night. In the last few years two other drugs, famcyclovir (trade name Famvir) and valacyclovir (Valtrex) have been developed; they retain more of their power when they are absorbed, and require only three doses a day, taken every eight hours. They work a little differently from acyclovir because they are *prodrugs*, which are chemically converted to active form during the absorption process.

46

How Shingles Is Treated

The course of treatment for all these drugs is a period of seven days, which experiments have shown to produce the best results.

Virtually all drugs may have negative side effects, but the side effects of these three antiviral drugs are usually no more than annoying. The most common are headache and digestive-tract irritations—nausea, and either constipation or diarrhea. Less common, but occasional, is irritation of the kidneys from crystallization of the drug in the tubules.

In rare instances, the virus may be resistant to all three drugs. Another drug, foscarnet (brand name Foscavir), may then be substituted. It tends to be stronger, but more likely to cause harmful side effects—kidney damage, in particular.

Internal Painkillers

Painkilling drugs, ranging from mild, over-the-counter aspirin to strong narcotics, may not be capable of completely relieving shingles pain, but they can make it more tolerable, especially if used in combination with other methods. As mentioned earlier, they don't attack the underlying cause of shingles, only its symptoms. They fall into four main categories:

- *Nonsteroidal anti-inflammatory drugs* (NSAIDs), such as aspirin and ibuprofen.

- *Acetominophen*, of which the best known form is Tylenol.

- *Narcotics*, also known as opioids.

- *Corticosteroids*, sometimes called simply steroids.

Each of these types reduces pain in somewhat different ways.

How Shingles Is Treated

NSAIDs: Nonsteroidal anti-inflammatory drugs have an awkward name, and they get it from what they aren't. That is, they aren't steroids. But they have one main effect in common with steroids: they relieve inflammation. Inflammation is a common reaction of cells to damage by injury or disease. The damaged cells release a variety of chemicals, some of which either stimulate pain-sensing neurons directly, or make them more sensitive to repeated stimulation (by lowering the pain threshold). Anti-inflammatory drugs block the production of one variety of these chemicals, the prostaglandins.

NSAIDs also have an effect that steroids don't. In ways not completely understood, they appear to relieve the perception of pain in the central nervous system—the spinal column and the brain.

So NSAIDs are doubly useful in treating shingles. They relieve the inflammation caused by the virus in nerve and skin cells, and they also reduce the sensation of pain, which in neurogenic conditions like shingles can be very intense.

By far the best known and most widely used NSAID is aspirin, technically known as acetylsalicylic acid, or A.S.A. The second best known is ibuprofen, familiar under such brand names as Advil, Motrin, and Nuprin. Aspirin and ibuprofen are the only NSAIDs available over the counter; all the others require a prescription. There are several of them, including diflusinal (trade name Dolobid),

49

indomethacin (Indocin), naproxen (Naprocyn), and piroxicam (Feldene). The effectiveness of individual drugs can differ considerably from one person to another. You might have to try more than one to find the one that works best for you.

NSAIDs have some potentially adverse side effects, especially when taken in large doses by older people. The most serious of these is irritation of the stomach lining, which may lead to ulcers and bleeding. The stomach contains powerful digestive acids, from which it is normally protected by a coating of mucus. The formation of mucus requires stimulation by prostaglandins, but NSAIDs hinder the production of prostaglandins. Lower levels of prostaglandins mean less mucus; less mucus means more acid irritation of the lining.

One real danger is that the irritation may not be noticeable, and the resulting bleeding may become severe. Moreover, it may be compounded by another side effect. NSAIDs—aspirin in particular—interfere with the activity of blood components called platelets, which are largely responsible for blood clotting. So, if the irritation does result in bleeding, the bleeding may be hard to stop. (And, by the way, the irritation may be intensified by alcohol. Even moderate drinking while taking NSAIDs may be risky.)

The stomach irritation can be somewhat reduced by taking NSAIDs that are covered with an enteric coating, which dissolves only after the tablet passes from the stomach to the small intestine. NSAIDs can also be taken with an antacid buffer to neutralize stomach acid, or the production of acid can be reduced with an antiulcer and antiheartburn drug such as Tagamet or Pepcid. But none of these expedients will completely remove the risk.

NSAIDs can cause allergic reactions in sensitive individuals. They may also interfere with normal central nervous system functions, especially in older people. Possible symptoms include headaches, dizziness, drowsiness, and mental confusion. Long-term NSAID use may hinder the ability of the kidneys to process wastes.

None of these adverse side effects are as likely to occur if NSAIDs are taken in modest doses for a short period of time. But the pain of shingles may require fairly strong dosage, and it may linger for weeks or even months. Bottom line: you and your doctor should closely monitor the use of these drugs, and it may be advisable to test occasionally for traces of blood in your stool.

Acetominophen: Acetominophen is second only to aspirin in its popularity as an analgesic. It is probably better known to most people under such brand names as Tylenol, Datril, and Panadol. It is also combined with aspirin in such formulations as Excedrin Extra Strength and Vanquish.

51

Acetominophen does not reduce inflammation. It apparently operates only upon the central nervous system, altering the perception of pain. It is comparable to aspirin as an analgesic, and many people prefer it because it has fewer adverse side effects. It doesn't irritate the stomach lining or hinder blood clotting, and it seldom causes allergic reactions. Large doses, however, may eventually damage the liver or kidneys.

Narcotics: The formal name for narcotics is *opioids*. Medical people prefer that term, because it doesn't smack of lawbreaking and addiction. But it is also more accurate, for it literally means "resembling opium." And indeed, the opioids are all closely related to that ancient pain remedy. They are either derived from it, or chemically similar to it, and they relieve pain in the same way.

Opioids imitate and reinforce the action of chemicals that exist naturally in the central nervous system. Among the functions of these chemicals is to inhibit the transmission of pain sensations among the neurons. For the relief of severe, persistent pain, opioids are in a class by themselves; no other drugs are anywhere near so effective.

Opioids have other effects on the nervous system as well—effects that are both positive and negative.

- They affect the nerves that control the contractions of the intestines, slowing them down. This feature makes them very useful in controlling diarrhea, but it can also cause constipation.

- They can stimulate the central nervous system center that triggers nausea and vomiting.

- They reduce the activity of the cough center in the brain. A mild opioid like codeine makes a good cough remedy. But since coughing helps clear the air passages, suppressing it can complicate breathing disorders such as asthma or emphysema.

- They depress the central respiratory drive, reducing the rate and depth of breathing. This effect, too, may intensify breathing disorders, and an overdose can lead to respiratory arrest.

- They cause blood vessels to dilate, which makes them useful in treating heart attacks. But dilation also contributes to hypotension, an abrupt lowering of the blood pressure that can provoke fainting.

- They act as sedatives, generally reducing the activity of the central nervous system. Sedation reinforces pain relief, but it can also lead to drowsiness, impaired alertness, and loss of coordination.

- Finally, they affect parts of the brain associated with the emotions, diminishing anxiety and producing euphoria. Reducing anxiety helps relieve pain, but euphoria can contribute to dependence.

That's why many doctors are reluctant to prescribe opioids for any extended period, and why many patients are reluctant to take them, or feel guilty if they do. They fear that the use of any of these drugs will lead to dependence and addiction. The fear is mistaken. Opioids taken to relieve pain are very unlikely to produce euphoria, and virtually never lead to the compulsive craving of addiction. Although the process isn't well understood, opioids seem to be targeted toward the pain sensation, and their other effects on the nervous system are reduced. Furthermore, when opioids are administered under medical supervision, the doses can be controlled to minimize increased tolerance and dependence. People in pain shouldn't be denied these valuable drugs out of a baseless fear that they will become addicts.

Opioids are not prescribed for shingles unless the pain is fairly severe. They can be especially helpful when taken at bedtime, since they not only relieve pain but induce drowsiness. They are often combined with aspirin or acetominophen. A mild form, such as codeine or propoxyphene (Darvon), is usually enough to produce satisfactory relief. Seldom is a stronger drug such as meperidine (Demerol) or oxycodone (Percocet, Percodan) needed, unless shingles develops into post-herpetic neuralgia.

Corticosteroids: Corticosteroids are natural hormones produced in the outer layer, or cortex, of the adrenal glands. Corticosteroid drugs are derived from the natural hormones, or resemble them chemically. For convenience, they are often simply called steroids, but they shouldn't be confused with *anabolic* steroids, used (and abused) by athletes to bulk up their muscles and improve their performance.

Corticosteroid drugs, such as prednisone and triamcinolone, have powerful anti-inflammatory effects. Like NSAIDs, only more so, they hinder the formation of prostaglandins. But their use in treating shingles is highly controversial. They have several potentially harmful side effects. Like NSAIDs, for example, they trigger irritation, ulcers, and bleeding of the stomach lining. And they have other potentially harmful side effects that NSAIDs don't. Taken in large doses over an extended period, they raise the risks of elevated blood pressure (hypertension), bone weakening (osteoporosis), swelling of the ankles from fluid retention (edema), and diabetes. Moreover, they tend to suppress the body's immune system. Thus, even though they may relieve the symptoms of shingles, they may at the same time reinforce one of the underlying causes of the disease. Some doctors feel that the benefits of the drugs outweigh the drawbacks, especially when the symptoms are severe, or when there is a risk of serious complications, such as eye damage (see Chapter 5). But many avoid prescribing corticosteroids for this purpose, especially in treating older patients.

Topical Medications

Many skin diseases are treated with topical medications—lotions, creams, ointments, and the like, applied directly to the skin. Their usefulness in relieving shingles is limited, however, because the pain of shingles results from damage to the sensory nerves, and not just from irritation of the skin. Nonetheless, some of them appear to provide at least partial relief, especially when used with other forms of treatment.

Bathing: Technically, soap and water can't be considered a topical medication. But bathing regularly and keeping the inflamed area as clean as possible can not only have a soothing effect, but can also reduce the risk of bacterial infection, especially when the blisters begin to break open.

Wet Dressings and Compresses: A very simple but sometimes effective topical treatment is a wet cloth, applied as a dressing or compress to the inflamed area for ten minutes or so at a time, several times a day. The cloth may be soaked in plain lukewarm water, or a solution of salt or baking soda.

57

LIVING WITH SHINGLES

Another traditional remedy is a dressing or compress soaked in a solution of aluminum acetate (Burow's solution). It acts as an astringent, firming and drying the skin, and apparently helps draw out some of the irritants (such as prostaglandins) that trigger pain.

Anti-itch Medications (Antiprurients): When one of the symptoms of shingles is intense itching, topical anti-itch medications (known formally as antiprurients) may give relief. One of the most familiar is calamine lotion, based on zinc oxide and ferric oxide. It is sometimes supplemented with cooling agents such as menthol, phenol, or camphor. Other antiprurients used for shingles include doxepin (Zonalon) and tolamine salicylate (Aspercreme). Antiprurients that are *not* generally used for this purpose are the topical corticosteroids. They have fewer harmful side effects than corticosteroids taken internally (see above), but tend to make the skin thinner and more fragile.

Topically Applied Aspirin: In a number of clinical experiments, crushed aspirin tablets mixed into an evaporating fluid carrier and dabbed on shingles rash have proved effective in relieving pain. In the original experiments the aspirin powder was mixed with chloroform. (Note: Don't try this at home!) But lotions such as Vaseline Intensive Care, or even rubbing alcohol or witch hazel, can be substituted.

Topical Anesthetics: Topical anesthetics not only relieve pain, they blunt all sensation by producing numbness. Their effects may not last very long, but they may nevertheless provide very welcome temporary relief. Among those used to treat shingles are lidocaine and pramoxine, under various trade names.

Topical Antibiotics and Antibacterials: As we've said before, antibiotics and other antibacterial drugs don't attack viruses. But if your doctor is concerned that your blisters might be infected by bacteria when they break open, you might be prescribed a topical antibiotic such as bacitracin or an antibacterial such as silver sulfadiazine, for extra protection.

Incidentally, it is wise to let blisters open up by themselves. Breaking them open by pricking them, scratching them, or pinching them increases the risk of infection.

LIVING WITH SHINGLES

Stress Management

Many people who have shingles notice that the pain may be triggered or intensified by psychological stress. The link between shingles pain and stress has important implications for treatment. Simple techniques for stress management can powerfully reinforce the effects of drugs and other medical agents.

Controlled Breathing: Often the best way to control psychological stress is physical relaxation. But achieving relaxation may require more than simply willing your body to relax, especially if you are in pain. Relaxation exercises, practiced until they become habitual, may help. One of the simplest is controlled breathing. Many people find it to be an "instant tranquilizer," which reduces physical tension and induces mental calm. It is also unobtrusive—you can do it almost anywhere, anytime.

The controlled breathing exercise has four steps:

1. Either sit or lie down in a comfortable, relaxed position. If necessary, loosen your collar so there is no constriction around your neck.

2. Inhale slowly and deeply through your nose. Concentrate on breathing into your abdomen, not just your chest. Count up to five at one-second intervals. Between each count, think of a single word, such as "calm" or "peace," to help free your mind of distracting or stressful thoughts.

3. Hold your breath without tension or stress for one second. Then exhale slowly through your mouth, counting backward from five to one, silently repeating your chosen word. At the same time, let your chest and stomach muscles relax, and drop your shoulders.

4. Repeat this cycle at least three times, but continue the process for three to five minutes if you can. If the extra oxygen makes you feel light-headed, alternate a few shallow breaths with the deep breaths.

Progressive Relaxation: Controlled breathing can be followed up with a more extended exercise called progressive relaxation. This exercise is usually performed by successively tensing and relaxing groups of muscles in specific parts of the body, starting at the feet and ending at the head. However, *this procedure may not be advisable if you have shingles.* Tensing the muscles, particularly in the affected area, may in fact produce a pain attack. You can try a purely mental form of the exercise, in which you concentrate on each group of muscles in turn, allowing them to relax while forming an image in your mind of warmth and heaviness.

Either way, the progressive relaxation sequence typically consists of focusing on the muscle groups in each of the following parts of the body:

- The toes of each foot
- Each foot as a whole
- The calf of each leg
- The thigh of each leg
- The buttocks
- The stomach
- The shoulders
- Each upper arm
- Each lower arm and hand
- The neck
- The face
- The forehead and top of the head

When the sequence is complete, the whole body should be allowed to relax while you form a mental image of sinking, going limp, and letting go. Like controlled breathing, this exercise should be practiced at least once a day until it becomes a habit. Some people find it especially helpful at bedtime, to help them fall asleep.

Meditation: While relaxation exercises help manage psychological stress by altering its physical expression, techniques of distraction work upon it directly. They are intended to relieve anxiety and the perception of pain by distracting the sufferer's attention away from them. Probably the best-known and most ancient form of distraction is meditation.

Meditation has its roots in Asian religion and philosophy. Its traditional functions are to separate the mind from the limits of ordinary reality and to achieve inner peace. But it can also reduce stress and pain, and it can be performed easily, without any special training or grounding in either philosophy or religion. The technique requires only a quiet environment and repeated practice. Here are its basic steps:

1. Select a word or phrase that has pleasant, tranquil connotations for you. Always use the same word or phrase so that you will automatically associate it with the calming, restorative effect of meditation.

2. Either sit or lie down in a comfortable, relaxed position, and close your eyes.

3. Breathe slowly and naturally. Each time you exhale, repeat your chosen word.

4. Let your mind become otherwise empty and passive. If distracting thoughts intrude, try gently to disregard them.

5. Continue for at least ten minutes.

Once the procedure has become familiar and habitual, even a quiet environment may become unnecessary. Many people use meditation to create an island of tranquility in the midst of stressful surroundings.

Guided Imagery: Imagination can powerfully affect perception and feeling. The technique of guided imagery uses imagination to distract attention from stressful, unpleasant circumstances (such as pain) and to substitute a relaxing, agreeable environment in their place.

You begin by developing a mental image of a pleasant, tranquil scene—a favorite getaway in the

64

mountains or at the beach, for example. You then try to direct your whole attention to that scene, immersing yourself in its details and experiencing it with all your senses. At least once a day, set aside time to recall this image, until you can do so easily at will. You can then use guided imagery to distance yourself from stress and the perception of pain. The technique has, in fact, been described as "taking a vacation from pain."

Sensory Substitution: Unlike other techniques of distraction, sensory substitution is aimed directly at the sensation of pain. Instead of trying to divert your attention entirely away from pain, you imagine that some other nonpainful sensation has been substituted for it, such as coolness or mild prickling. This method may sound difficult, and it does require determination and practice. But some people find that it provides significant relief, particularly from pain in a specific, circumscribed area—shingles pain, for example.

Other Methods of Treatment

There are a couple of techniques for treating shingles pain that don't quite fit into any of the categories we have discussed, but which have proved helpful to some patients.

Counterirritation: When you scratch an itch or vigorously rub a barked shin, you are making use of a natural, almost instinctive method of relieving irritation and pain, called counterirritation. The mildly irritating sensations produced by scratching and rubbing are transmitted to the central nervous system, where they trigger reactions that diminish the sensations of itching and pain.

Some people find counterirritation methods useful in reducing the pain and itching of shingles. Incidentally, scratching is *not* one of them; breaking open the blisters raises the risk of bacterial infection. But for some people just massaging the affected area with a towel brings at least partial and temporary relief. Some find it easier to get to sleep if they bind the area with an elastic sports bandage at bedtime. And some also are helped by rubefacient ("red-making") liniments and ointments, containing oil of win-

66

tergreen or menthol. These dilate the blood vessels, causing the skin to flush and feel warm, but they also seem to work as counterirritants to the transmission of pain sensations.

TENS: A technique that is often used in the treatment of joint and muscle pain is also occasionally used to relieve shingles. It is called *transcutaneous electrical nerve stimulation*, or TENS for short. A portable machine produces mild pulses of electrical current, which pass through electrodes to the skin, provoking a tingling sensation (transcutaneous means "across the skin").

Just how TENS relieves pain isn't known. Counterirritation may be involved. But it does appear to be helpful in some cases, and the low-energy electrical current is quite harmless.

Conclusion

Mark Singer's rash, as his doctor had predicted, subsided in about a week. Not only was he pleased that his attack was so mild, he was also thankful that his chances of getting shingles again were greatly reduced. His doctor told him that only about one in twenty people who had shingles later went through another attack.

Susan MacDonald began taking antiviral medication the same day she saw her dermatologist. She also applied wet compresses of Burow's solution to the affected area, and took a combination of aspirin and codeine at bedtime to help her sleep. In four days she felt considerably better, but at the insistence of her doctor continued to take the antiviral drug for the full seven days of the prescription. She also continued to find the wet compresses soothing, but soon switched from aspirin and codeine to plain aspirin and then to nothing at all. In three weeks, the rash was completely gone, and ten days after that, she no longer noticed any pain at all. She, too, was pleased to learn from her doctor that she was unlikely to suffer a recurrence.

How Shingles Is Treated

After taking an antiviral drug for a week, Fred Weintraub didn't feel noticeably better. He took meperidine and acetinophen three times a day, and got some relief from applying an anesthetic ointment every few hours. Two weeks later, the rash began to heal, but the pain lingered on. He had trouble sleeping, and also suffered from loss of appetite.

His doctor shared Fred's disappointment. "I'm afraid you have post-herpetic neuralgia," he said.

Fortunately, most people recover completely from shingles within a few weeks, and antiviral drugs and other treatments help considerably to relieve its symptoms. Furthermore, once they have recovered, they have only about a one in twenty chance of suffering another attack in their lifetimes. Apparently the reactivation of the virus also strengthens the immune system to keep it in check.

But some people, especially those older than seventy-five, are not so lucky. The acute stage of the disease is likely to be more severe, and is more likely to be followed by the most unpleasant condition called post-herpetic neuralgia. We will discuss this condition and its treatment in the next chapter.

CHAPTER 4

Post-Herpetic Neuralgia

Fred Weintraub was deeply disappointed and distressed by the persistence of deep burning pain more than two weeks after the last of his shingles rash disappeared. He was further upset by the gradual appearance of another disturbing symptom. Any light, brushing touch upon the skin in and around the shingles area produced spasms of sharp, stabbing pain. It felt as if a cat were sharpening its claws on his back and chest. He spent his days stripped to the waist to avoid the friction of his clothes, and went to bed at night without a pajama top or even a sheet over him.

LIVING WITH SHINGLES

"I want you to try some different medications," his dermatologist said. "As best as we can tell, post-herpetic neuralgia is a rather different condition from shingles."

"Could have fooled me," Fred grumbled. "Feels like the same thing, only worse."

"True," the doctor acknowledged. "But at this stage, other kinds of treatment seem to be more helpful."

"Will they cure the pain?"

"For most people, they seem to cut the time it lasts, or at least make it more tolerable. But I don't want to offer any false promises. There's a lot we don't understand about this problem."

Just When You Thought It Was Over

After the rash of shingles has healed and the herpes zoster virus is no longer active, you might expect the pain to subside as well. For younger people with relatively strong immune systems, that is indeed what happens. But for a substantial number of older patients, the pain doesn't end. It either persists or returns after a short interval, and it can be as bad as, or worse than, the original attack. This is the complication of shingles known as post-herpetic neuralgia.

There is no common, informal name for post-herpetic neuralgia, other than the initials PHN. The medical name may seem rather clumsy, but it is at least accurate. The condition is indeed post-herpetic—it occurs only *after* acute herpes zoster and is a direct consequence of it. And the main symptom is neuralgia—literally, "nerve pain"—which arises mainly within the nerves themselves.

Overall, one person will suffer PHN out of every three that have shingles. But the ratio varies enormously depending on age. PHN is very rare among shingles patients less than forty years old, unless their immune systems are very weak. But by age sixty, the risk of developing PHN after shingles rises to fifty percent. At age seventy, it reaches seventy-five per-cent. In short, the older you are when you have shin-gles, the more likely you are to suffer PHN afterward.

It is hard to predict exactly who will get PHN, or how severe it will be, or how long it will last. It seems to occur more often among those whose shingles symptoms were relatively severe, and particularly among those who experienced noticeable pain before the shingles rash appeared. For some, the neuralgia is a mild annoyance; for others, an unrelenting, dis-abling agony. The majority recover within a few months. But some continue to have pain for a year or more, and, again, the percentage rises with age. For a small number—fortunately, very small—the pain continues indefinitely.

Symptoms

With one significant exception, the symptoms of PHN are similar to those of shingles:

Burning Pain: The most common symptom is a deep, burning pain, essentially the same as that of shingles, and typical of neurogenic pain in general.

Partial Numbness: As in shingles, the skin may be at least partly numb to external stimuli, such as heat, pressure, vibration, or even the prick of a pin. The numb area may extend outside the area of the shingles rash.

Allodynia: Allodynia is the exception we mentioned. It is a mysterious and very distressing symptom, which is far more typical of PHN than it is of shingles. The term comes from Greek words meaning "other" and "force." Allodynia is a spasm of stabbing pain, triggered by some other sensation that is not in itself painful. Often the sensation is a light, moving touch across the skin, of the sort that can be

75

caused by the friction of clothes or bedding, or by a light breeze. When the affected area is on the face, simple activities like brushing the teeth, shaving, or combing the hair may provoke pain. Other potential triggers of allodynia include heat, cold, and sunlight. In some fashion, not well understood, these harmless sensations, transmitted through nerves that don't normally sense pain, somehow trigger the nerves in the pain pathways.

Like numbness, allodynia may occur in areas outside those of the shingles rash.

Other Effects: Perhaps even more so than shingles, PHN can be physically and emotionally debilitating— simply because of its persistence. Common symptoms include insomnia, loss of appetite, apathy and social withdrawal, depression, and obsessive preoccupation with pain.

Causes

There is no disagreement about what causes shingles—it results from reactivation of the chickenpox virus. By contrast, there is no agreement, and considerable controversy, about what causes PHN.

On certain points, most experts do agree. Once the rash has healed, the virus is no longer active and no longer the basic source of pain. PHN apparently arises from damage to the sensory nerves—not only the peripheral nerves that carry sensations from the skin to the spinal cord, but also the nerves of the spinal cord itself. And the affected nerves of the central nervous system are not only those that carry sensations through the spinal cord to the brain, but also those that control and modulate the strength of those sensations. But just how this damage is transformed into the pain and abnormal sensations of PHN is not at all clear. The mechanism of allodynia, in which pain-sensing nerves and other sensory nerves somehow interact, is especially mystifying.

Goals of Treatment

Post-herpetic neuralgia is notoriously difficult to treat. Some of the drugs used to relieve shingles appear to be ineffective against this disorder. No drug or other remedy offers more than partial relief, and none provides a complete cure. Moreover, individual response to different forms of treatment varies widely. Finding an effective approach must often be a process of trial and error.

Nonetheless, some methods do seem to be helpful, at least in achieving the two basic goals of treatment:

- Reducing pain to at least tolerable levels.

- Significantly shortening the course of the disease.

These goals may seem disappointingly modest. Perhaps they are. But at the present point of medical progress, they are the best you can hope for. And they are more than you could have hoped for just a decade or so ago.

What Doesn't Work

Some types of pain treatment—including some of those used to treat shingles—appear to offer either less help or none at all against PHN.

Antiviral Drugs: Antiviral drugs, such as acyclovir, famcyclovir, and valacyclovir, are demonstrably effective in reducing the intensity and shortening the course of shingles. Statistical studies indicate that they also tend to reduce the incidence of PHN and shorten the time needed to recover from it, possibly by diminishing the amount of nerve damage that the active virus causes. But antiviral drugs are only helpful at the very early stage of shingles, when they prevent the virus from reproducing further. They have no direct effect on PHN, and aren't used in treating it.

Analgesics: Over-the-counter painkillers such as aspirin, acetaminophen (Tylenol, etc.), and ibuprofen offer little or no relief from PHN. Neither do prescription nonsteroidal anti-inflammatory drugs (NSAIDs) such as indomethacin (Indocin) or naproxen (Naprocyn).

79

The only exception is aspirin applied *topically* to the skin (see below).

Corticosteroids: Using anti-inflammatory cortico-steroids for PHN is, if anything, even more contro-versial than using them for shingles. Some medical authorities believe that they are completely ineffec-tive. Many others believe that their potential side effects are too dangerous, especially for older patients, to justify their use.

Acupuncture: Acupuncture has a long tradition of use in treating pain, and some people maintain that it has helped them overcome PHN. But statistical studies conclude that it is largely ineffective for this purpose.

Narcotics: Narcotics, technically known as opioids, appear to be much less effective in relieving the pain of PHN than they are in relieving shingles. They are gen-erally prescribed only when other approaches don't work. However, as we've said before, there need be no hesitation in using opioids to relieve pain. If you take them under medical supervision, you face little risk of dependency.

Antidepressants

Impulses are passed from one neuron (nerve cell) to another by chemicals called neurotransmitters. Antidepressant drugs cause certain neurotransmitters to remain active for longer than they ordinarily would, thus strengthening the communication among the neurons they serve. Antidepressants, as the name indicates, are mainly used to relieve psychological depression. They influence the activity of neurotransmitters in the parts of the brain that process emotions.

But one type, known as tricyclic antidepressants, has also proved useful in the treatment of neurogenic pain—such as PHN. They apparently enhance the activity of spinal nerves that hinder the transmission of pain impulses to the brain. In recent years, just as antiviral drugs have become leading tools in relieving shingles, tricyclic antidepressants have become leading tools in relieving PHN.

For many people, the most effective of these drugs appears to be amitriptyline (brand names Elavil and Endep). But, as we've said, individual reactions vary, and some patients may find that other drugs, such as nortriptyline, desipramine, or maprotiline, work better. (Maprotiline isn't a tricyclic, but its chemistry is very similar).

LIVING WITH SHINGLES

Incidentally, there are other antidepressants besides the tricyclics. Probably the most familiar of these are fluoxetine (Prozac) and sertraline (Zoloft). But they act in different ways upon neurotransmitters, and don't work as well against the pain of PHN.

As a rule, far lower doses of antidepressants are used in treating PHN than in treating depression. Most experts recommend that treatment begin promptly—when the shingles rash disappears but the pain persists. It may take days or even weeks for relief to become noticeable. And not all patients—only about two in three—are significantly helped.

Antidepressants also affect other parts of the nervous system, producing side effects that tend to be annoying rather than dangerous. Probably the most common of these is dryness of the mouth, caused by diminished salivation. It can be relieved with sprays of artificial saliva, but drinking more water or sucking on fruit drops may work about as well. Another common side effect is constipation, which can generally be relieved by bulk laxatives or stool softeners. Other possible problems include "cold" sweating, susceptibility to fainting, drowsiness, heart palpitations, and weight gain from increased appetite.

Anticonvulsants

While the most typical symptom of PHN is deep, burning pain, it may be accompanied by spasms of stabbing pain, either spontaneous, or triggered by nonpainful sensations (allodynia). These spasms are apparently caused by the uncontrolled, abnormal firing of pain-sensing neurons. They are therefore sometimes treated with anticonvulsant drugs—the drugs used to control the abnormal firing of brain cells that produces the convulsions of epilepsy. Anticonvulsants are also used in the treatment of another neurogenic pain disorder: trigeminal neuralgia, which causes pain in the face.

The drug most commonly used to treat PHN is carbamazepine (Tegretol), but others include phenytoin (Dilantin), valproic acid (Depakene), and gabapentin (Neurontin). Among their possible side effects are dizziness, drowsiness, blurred vision, and nausea.

NMDA Blockers

Research continues for drugs that might relieve PHN. A number of approaches are being taken in the lab, but one particular group that seems to have at least theoretical promise is that of the NMDA blockers.

As we've said, neurons convey impulses from one to another by means of chemical neurotransmitters. A stimulated neuron generates neurotransmitters at its output end, and these chemicals cross the gap, or synapse, to the next neuron, attaching themselves to receptors there, and stimulating them to fire in turn.

Among the chemical receptors of pain-sensing neurons are those with the jaw-breaking name of N-methyl-D-aspartate receptors—NMDA for short. Drugs that block NMDA receptors are believed to slow or stop the transmission of pain sensations to the brain.

The only NMDA blocker now legally available is dextromethorphan (although it has been postulated that nitrous oxide relieves pain by blocking NMDA receptors). It is an ingredient in cough remedies, for it also acts upon the cough center in the brain.

Post-Herpetic Neuralgia

So far, its effects on pain have proved disappointing. But researchers hope that others of this type can be developed that will achieve better results.

Topical Medications

Some of the topical medications (lotions, ointments, etc.) that are used to treat shingles are also helpful in relieving PHN. They may provide only temporary and partial relief, but that relief can be very welcome. In general, they are easy to apply and have relatively few side effects.

In addition, there is one topical medication, capsaicin, that is specifically intended for treating PHN.

Topical Anesthetics: Topical ointments containing such anesthetics as lidocaine, and pramoxine numb the skin where they are applied. One preparation that has proved helpful to many patients is EMLA (eutetic mixture of local anesthetics), which is a cream containing lidocaine and prilocaine. The effects of topical anesthetics may last no more than a few hours, but they may provide significant relief when it particularly matters—at bedtime, for example, when you're trying to get to sleep.

Topically Applied Aspirin: As we've said, aspirin taken internally seems to be of little or no help against

PHN. But crushed aspirin tablets, mixed into an evaporating carrier and applied to the affected skin, do seem to provide meaningful relief for at least some patients.

Capsaicin: Capsaicin is the active ingredient that makes hot peppers hot. For medicinal use, it is mixed into an ointment, marketed under such brand names as Zostrix, Dolorac, and Capzacin. Applied to the skin, it produces a burning, stinging sensation, which is followed by at least some reduction in sensitivity to pain. It is believed that capsaicin lowers the level of a neurotransmitter called substance P, which facilitates the transmission of pain impulses to the spinal nerves and brain.

But capsaicin doesn't work for everyone. A few authorities question whether it works at all. It must be applied very carefully to the face, for it must be kept away from the eyes. And it has one other big drawback: it takes a good deal of getting used to. Just as you have to desensitize your mouth by repeatedly eating mild peppery dishes before you can take on a really hot chili, so, too, do you have to apply capsaicin repeatedly before the initial stinging sensation subsides. And many people just can't bear it for that long. It may help, during the period of acclimatization, to apply a numbing topical anesthetic *before* rubbing in the capsaicin.

87

LIVING WITH SHINGLES

Topical Rubefacients: Those who can't tolerate cap-saicin may be helped by milder liniments or oint-ments, based upon oil of wintergreen or menthol. Probably the most familiar brand is Ben-Gay. They are known as rubefacients ("red-makers"), for they dilate the blood vessels, causing the skin to flush and feel warm. But they also seem to work as counterirri-tants, which inhibit the transmission of pain sensa-tions through the nerves.

Electrical Stimulation

Just why low-level pulses of electrical current should give relief from pain is unknown, but they are nonetheless sometimes effective. The simplest method for delivering such pulses is called transcutaneous electrical nerve stimulation, or TENS for short. It is used for shingles as well as PHN. Electrodes from a portable generator are attached to affected areas on the skin (transcutaneous means "across the skin"), provoking tingling sensations and some measure of pain relief.

Much more intrusive is a method used occasionally to counteract long-persisting, intractable pain. Electrodes are surgically inserted through the base of the skull into parts of the brain. Electrical current transmitted between them seems to block the process of pain perception. The procedure appears to be very effective for some patients who haven't been helped by other methods. But nobody knows just how it works.

Psychological Approaches

One of the most unfortunate aspects of persistent, or chronic, pain is what is called the "pain cycle." Physical pain provokes psychological stress, which in turn intensifies the perception of pain, which leads to more stress, and so on. Furthermore, intense, unrelieved pain can do extensive psychological damage; it can, for example, lead or contribute to disabling depression and helpless invalidism. So psychological treatment can often be very helpful in breaking the pain cycle and in coping with both physical and emotional distress. It cannot replace drugs in the relief of PHN, but can substantially reinforce them.

Stress Management: The simplest psychological approaches are basic techniques for managing stress, which can be undertaken by just about anyone. They are also useful in relieving shingles, and have been discussed in more detail in the preceding chapter.

They fall into two categories. One is composed of techniques for relieving psychological tension by means of physical relaxation. Such techniques include exercises in controlled breathing and progressive relaxation of muscle groups.

90

Post-Herpetic Neuralgia

The second category is distraction. Its techniques are intended to relieve anxiety and pain perception by distracting the sufferer's attention away from them. The techniques include meditation, guided imagery, and sensory substitution.

Biofeedback: Biofeedback is a technique that is most often used in treating chronic headaches, but some people have also found it helpful in relieving PHN. It might be described as mechanically assisted relaxation.

A biofeedback machine is essentially an amplifier of weak electrical signals, received from electrodes attached to the skin. The electrodes register physical signs of stress—slight muscle contractions, for example, or changing levels of skin temperature—as electrical impulses. The biofeedback amplifier then strengthens the impulses and makes them either visible (flashing lights or a moving dial) or audible (tones, beeps, or clicks). The higher the level of tension, the more pronounced are the generated impulses, and the stronger is the visible or audible output.

The biofeedback machine doesn't really *do* anything to you, except to inform you how your body is responding to stress. But apparently when you become more aware of stress, you are better able to control it and to achieve relaxation. Through repeated biofeedback sessions, you may be able to retrain your nervous system to manage stress more success-fully, breaking into the pain cycle.

Hypnosis: Hypnosis is an artificially induced state of consciousness—a trance—in which your attention becomes tightly focused, and you become strongly susceptible to suggestion. Suggestion under hypnosis can greatly alter perception—including the perception of pain.

Just as biofeedback can be used to reinforce physical relaxation, hypnotism can be used to reinforce psychological distraction. Hypnotic suggestion can be used to make a part of your body numb—as if it were injected with an anesthetic. It can also be used to reduce the pain experience, transforming it into some other sensation (sensory substitution), or diminishing its emotional impact. And the effects of suggestion during a hypnotic trance may persist after you emerge from the trance—a phenomenon called posthypnotic suggestion.

But hypnotism has one big limitation. Many people can't be hypnotized at all, and many more can't achieve a deep enough level of trance to make suggestion fully effective. Only a minority can be easily and deeply hypnotized. The usefulness of the technique in relieving pain is largely confined to that minority.

Post-Herpetic Neuralgia

Cognitive Psychotherapy and Behavioral Therapy: If you are among the unfortunate few who suffer post-herpetic pain for a long period of time, you might find cognitive psychotherapy or behavioral therapy beneficial. These forms of treatment may not directly relieve your pain, but they may help keep it from intensifying. Perhaps even more important, they may enable you to cope better with pain so that it doesn't completely disable you.

Cognitive psychotherapy is a relatively recent off-shoot of conventional psychotherapy, and shows particular promise in the treatment of chronic pain. Whereas conventional psychotherapy probes deeply into unconscious motivation through the analysis of dreams, early memories, and the like, cognitive psychotherapy concentrates on the here-and-now—the ideas and values that determine your reactions to pain. It aims to make you rethink these mental attitudes so that instead of reinforcing your suffering, they will encourage coping and healing.

One technique of cognitive therapy is to encourage you to substitute positive "coping statements" for negative ones. For instance, instead of saying to yourself, "My pain is unbearable, and I can't go on suffering this way," you might be encouraged to say, "This pain is hard to take, but I've coped with it so far, and I'll be able to cope with it in the future."

Another type of psychological treatment for long-standing pain is behavioral therapy. Like cognitive psychotherapy it concentrates upon the here-and-now—specifically, upon the effects pain has upon your day-to-day behavior. It aims to reduce negative "pain behavior," such as wincing, grimacing, physical inactivity, withdrawal, or appeals for sympathy, and to replace the negative behavior with positive coping behavior. It is believed that these changes will not only enable you to live a more normal life, but may also make you perceive pain less intensely.

Nerve Blocks

Nerve blocks, which completely stop the transmission of impulses, are used infrequently but occasionally to treat post-herpetic pain. As a rule, they are only used as a last resort, when the pain is severe and long lasting, and other approaches have failed. They have many potentially serious side effects, and even the most radical of them—completely severing the nerves—offers only temporary relief.

There are two main types: blocks of sensory nerves, and blocks of sympathetic ganglia.

Sensory Nerve Blocks: The simplest nerve blocks are those produced by local anesthetics, injected into the area of the affected nerves. Using a relatively low concentration of anesthetic often relieves pain without provoking complete numbness. But the effect wears off within hours. Anesthetic blocks are used more often to treat especially severe shingles pain, but sometimes they are used to relieve PHN, in an effort to interrupt the pain cycle.

To achieve prolonged sensory blocks, the nerves must be severed by surgery, or destroyed with chemicals, cold, or heat. The procedure may be performed on nerve roots near the spinal column, on sections of the spinal cord, or even in parts of the brain. Needless to say, this is an extremely invasive approach. It produces complete numbness and often interferes with normal function in the affected parts of the body.

Prolonged blocks may not provide permanent relief. After a few months, the nerves regenerate, or other nerves take over their work. But even temporary relief may be welcome, and the break in the pain cycle may lead to lasting pain reduction.

Sympathetic Nerve Blocks: The sympathetic nervous system is composed of nerves that control autonomic (literally "self-ruling") body functions, ranging from perspiration to blood pressure. The sympathetic nerves would seem to have nothing to do with the sensory nerves. But for some reason—perhaps because of certain neurotransmitters they generate—they can trigger or intensify pain sensations. Blocking them, either temporarily or for a prolonged period, can be particularly helpful in relieving neurogenic pain, such as PHN.

Sympathetic nerves come together in clusters, or ganglia, at certain points along each side of the spinal column. To relieve pain, a block is applied to the ganglion serving the affected part of the body. Like sensory nerve blocks, sympathetic blocks may be temporary or prolonged. Temporary blocks are achieved with a local anesthetic, prolonged blocks by chemical destruction of the nerves.

The side effects of sympathetic blocks tend to be less severe than those of sensory blocks, but some normal functions may be at least temporarily altered. Like sensory blocks, even prolonged sympathetic blocks do not give permanent relief.

Multidisciplinary Pain Clinics

Shingles is customarily treated by an individual physician—a family practitioner or a dermatologist; PHN is sometimes treated by a neurologist. But if your suffering from PHN is especially severe or long-lasting, you may find it helpful to seek treatment in a pain clinic. Such clinics, often associated with a teaching hospital or university medical school, offer comprehensive treatment using a team of experts that might include a neurologist, an anesthesiologist, a physical therapist, and a psychologist, among others. The team undertakes a thorough examination and diagnosis, and provides a systematic treatment plan—often involving several different forms of treatment at once.

The benefits of a pain clinic go beyond the collective expertise of the team members. The main goals are not only to reduce pain and speed your recovery, but also to help you restore and maintain normal function. The combination of physical and psychological approaches can help you cope with your condition and carry on with your life, even if you haven't yet completely recovered.

Recovery

Recovery from PHN is likely to be intermittent. Attacks of pain alternate with periods of relief, and the attacks gradually become shorter and less intense, while the pain-free periods become longer. The steady, burning, "background" pain may disappear either earlier or later than the spasms of allodynia. The whole process may extend over several months, and each recurrence of pain is likely to be both physically and emotionally distressing. But once the pattern of pain alternating with relief becomes established, you can at least be reassured that eventual recovery is on the way.

Fred Weintraub was prescribed both antidepressant and anticonvulsant drugs, but for two weeks he noticed little or no change in his condition. The steady burning pain continued, and the merest touch might trigger clawing, stabbing spasms of allodynia.

He got a little relief from the anesthetic ointment he had been taking during the shingles attack. He tried a capsaicin ointment his doctor prescribed, but stopped using it after a couple of days because it produced so much pain of its own that he couldn't bear to continue. He found that a controlled breathing exercise provided a little relief from the spasms of allodynia. He also found progressive relaxation helpful, especially when he was trying to get to sleep.

Overall, however, these remedies were very limited in their effects. Fred found himself constantly exhausted from both pain and lack of sleep, and he lost more than twelve pounds from an almost total loss of appetite. He didn't want to go out or see anyone, and became more and more depressed by his apparent lack of progress.

But then, a little more than two weeks after he started the course of antidepressant and anticonvulsant drugs, he began to experience short periods of relief from steady pain, and there were at least a few less attacks of stabbing pain. Three months after he had come down with shingles, he was noticeably improved. By six months, the burning pain had disappeared, and wearing clothes was no longer an agony. But the attacks of stabbing allodynia took another three more months to subside, and he still suffers a brief twinge every now and then. When this happens, he becomes terrified that the neuralgia may return, although his doctor assures him that this almost never happens.

Fred remains apprehensive, but thankful that his suffering didn't last any longer than it did. He has been hearing a lot of horror stories lately, about people his age whose pain has persisted for years. "I never dreamed," he says, "that shingles could make you so miserable."

CHAPTER 5

Other Complications of Shingles

After retiring from the library, Connie Persig remained an avid reader. When she was seventy-six, she one day experienced a severe, stabbing headache on one side of her forehead. She thought she was suffering from eyestrain and might need new glasses. So she went to see her optometrist for an eye test.

After testing her vision, the optometrist told her that there seemed to be no need for new glasses. "Mrs. Persig," he said, "your headache doesn't seem to come from eyestrain."

"What else could it be?" she asked.

101

"I'm not sure," he replied. "But how long have you had that rash at the tip of your nose?"

"Rash?" she asked. "I haven't noticed any rash. It must have just popped out."

"I don't want to worry you unnecessarily, but I think you should see your physician right away. An ophthalmologist, too. I think you may have shingles in that part of your face. And, if you do, there's a risk that your eye will be involved."

"Is that serious?"

"It could be very serious. But you have a much better chance of heading off trouble if you get immediate treatment."

Other Complications of Shingles

Herpes Zoster Ophthalmicus

The most common potential complication of shingles is post-herpetic neuralgia (see preceding chapter), but there are a number of others. The second most common is viral infection of the area of the face that includes the eye. Its formal name is herpes zoster opthalmicus. For convenience, it is shortened to HZO.

As we've explained before, shingles results from the reactivation of the chickenpox virus, usually in a single sensory nerve. Its distinctive rash then appears in the specific area of the skin (*dermatome*, or "skin slice") served by that nerve. HZO results from reactivation of the virus in one of the three branches of the trigeminal ("triplet") nerve that serves the side of the face. The trigeminal nerve is a cranial nerve, which connects to the brainstem within the skull (the cranium). The affected branch serves the area of the forehead, the nose, and (most important) the eye, so it is called the ophthalmic branch.

HZO is not uncommon. Although shingles occurs most often in the various dermatomes of the trunk, the dermatome of the ophthalmic branch is the most frequent *single* site of the disease. HZO is estimated to account for about 15 percent of all cases of shingles.

LIVING WITH SHINGLES

And in something over half of the cases of HZO, the virus directly affects the eye.

The risk factors for HZO are the same as those for shingles in general. The principal factor is advancing age and the weakened immune system that goes with it. Also at risk are those people whose immune systems have been weakened by diseases such as AIDS or by drugs such as those used in chemotherapy against cancer. It is weakened immunity that apparently allows the virus to "come out of hiding" in the nerve root and proliferate toward the skin.

Symptoms of HZO: As is true of shingles in general, the first signs of infection may be vague or even misleading. You might have a low fever, or suffer from nausea, or just feel vaguely "rotten." If you suffer from a burning or stabbing pain in one side of your head, you might think it is migraine or the result of eyestrain, and even a physician might think that is a symptom of some other disease, such as temporal arteritis (inflammation of an artery in the temple) or trigeminal neuralgia. Only the appearance of the distinctive rash makes diagnosis certain.

A patch of rash near the tip of the nose, called Hutchinson's sign, is considered strong evidence that the eye will eventually be affected. The sign isn't entirely reliable, however. Some people who show Hutchinson's sign recover from HZO without any

Other Complications of Shingles

effects on the eye, and some whose rash doesn't occur on the nose nonetheless suffer eye damage.

Potential Damage to the Eye: HZO is considered a particularly threatening form of shingles. The reason is simple: The eye is a relatively delicate organ, and especially susceptible to damage. Moreover, the damage may be irreversible, and if it is severe, it may cause the diminishment or complete loss of a crucial function—vision.

Virtually any part of eye may be affected by viral infection. The effects may become apparent early, during the period of acute infection, or they may be delayed weeks or even months after the rash has healed. Among the areas most commonly and most seriously affected are the following:

- **Eyelids**

  During the acute attack of HZO, the eyelids—particularly the upper one—often become red and swollen, to the extent that they may be nearly or completely shut. Or the upper lid may droop uncontrollably, a condition called *ptosis*. These conditions usually disappear when the acute attack ends. But if the inflammation is severe, the lids may become permanently damaged. Some of the lashes may be lost, and the lids may not close properly.

- **Conjunctiva and Sclera**
The conjunctiva is a thin, transparent mucous membrane, which covers and protects the white of the eye. The sclera include the white of the eye and other outer layers of the eyeball. The invading virus may cause inflammation of either or both of these tissues. The inflammation may be very painful, but usually subsides without causing permanent damage.

- **Cornea**
The cornea is a transparent window of tissue in the front of the eye, through which light must pass on its way to the pupil. If the cornea is damaged, the light may be distorted or at least partly blocked so that no clear image can be received.

  Inflammation of the cornea, or keratitis, is one of the most frequent consequences of HZO, and it can be very serious. In most instances it is painful but only temporary. But sometimes it leads, either directly or by secondary bacterial infection, to permanent ulceration or scarring that impairs vision.

- **Iris**

  The iris is a muscular ring that controls the amount of light passing through the pupil. It automatically adjusts to different light levels, dilating in dim twilight and contracting in the bright glare of day. The iris also contains the pigment that gives the eye its distinctive color. Severe inflammation, or *iritis*, may cause lasting damage. For example, it may prevent the iris from correctly adjusting to changes in light levels.

  But even more serious is the harm that iritis can do, indirectly, to other parts of the eye. For example, it can lead to the vision-threatening disorder called glaucoma. Behind the iris is the transparent lens, which focuses light into a sharp image on the retina at the back of the eye. Between the lens and the cornea are two interconnected chambers, separated by the doughnut-shaped iris. The chambers are filled with clear watery fluid, which is steadily generated within the eye and just as steadily drained out of it, so that the amount in the chambers remains steady. Severe iritis may block the drainage channels, and accumulating fluid in the chambers may exert enough pressure through the lens to raise the pressure in the jellylike fluid in the rest of the eyeball. This pressure may in turn gradually damage the optic nerve, which carries visual information from the retina to the brain. The eventual result may be limited, "tunnel" vision, or, in extreme cases, blindness in that eye.

- **Lens**
  Inflammation around the lens of the eye may produce a cloudy area, or cataract, within it. A small cataract may have no noticeable impact, but an extensive one can dim or even block vision.

- **Other Parts of the Eye**
  Viral inflammation inside the eyeball may directly damage the choroid lining, the retina, or the optic nerve. The damage may in turn have an impact on vision, ranging from mild to severe, and from passing to permanent.

- **Muscles Controlling Eye Movement**
  A network of muscles around each eye controls its movement and enables the

eyes to work together as a pair. Inflammation from HZO may damage the motor nerves controlling these muscles so that the affected eye can no longer coordinate properly with the normal one. The result may be blurry or double vision, which is usually only temporary.

Treatment of HZO: Because the possible effects of HZO can be so devastating, it is especially important to get treatment just as soon as the diagnosis becomes clear. In general, HZO is treated with the same methods used for other forms of shingles (see Chapter 3). But an ophthalmologist should be part of the professional team, to monitor for such adverse effects as glaucoma.

- **Antiviral Drugs**

  The most promising tools for treating HZO are the antiviral drugs—acyclovir, famcyclovir, and valacyclovir—used for other forms of shingles. The sooner they are taken, the better. If more than three days (seventy-two hours) go by after the outbreak of the rash, the chances are that the drugs won't be fully effective. If the inflammation is especially severe, it may be advisable to have acyclovir administered intravenously. This may be a great nuisance, but the stakes are high.

Antiviral drugs are best taken internally. Topical antivirals—drops and ointments—are available, but there is general agreement that they do little to relieve HZO. And there is virtually universal agreement that they are no substitute for the pills or injections.

- **Analgesics**

  Analgesics (painkillers)—especially non-steroidal anti-inflammatory drugs (NSAIDs), such as aspirin and ibuprofen—can be useful in reducing both the pain and the inflammation of HZO. Stronger drugs, such as narcotics (opioids), are seldom necessary.

- **Corticosteroids**

  The use of corticosteroid drugs for treating HZO is controversial, but less so for treating shingles at other sites. Because the consequences of severe eye inflammation are so potentially devastating, many opthamologists feel that the benefits of corticosteroids outweigh the risks, except in special instances such as severely immuno-

Other Complications of Shingles

suppressed patients. Corticosteroids can be applied topically or taken internally.

- **Lubricating Drops**
  Keeping the surface of the eye moist with lubricating drops or artificial tears can reduce irritation and promote healing.

- **Topical Antibiotics**
  Some ophthalmologists recommend applying topical antibiotic drops or ointments to the eyes to reduce the risk of secondary bacterial infection in the inflamed eyelids, conjunctiva, sclera, and cornea.

Treatment for the Consequences of HZO: Many of the adverse effects on the eye can be treated, if not completely remedied, with techniques that range from drugs to surgery.

- **Surgery**
  Damaged eyelids can often be repaired with plastic surgery. Damaged conjunctival membranes usually repair themselves, but if necessary they can sometimes be repaired surgically, or even replaced with transplants. Replacement with a human transplant is the standard

treatment for a badly damaged cornea. A lens with a severe cataract is now customarily replaced with an artificial substitute.

- **Treatment for Glaucoma**
  One of the main reasons for including an ophthalmologist in the treatment team is to watch for signs of glaucoma—particularly increased pressure within the eye. Glaucoma is mainly treated with drugs, many applied as eyedrops. Some of these drugs decrease the production of watery fluid in the chambers between the lens and the cornea. Others help to keep the drainage channels open. In severe cases, surgery may eventually become necessary to provide drainage.

Other Complications of Shingles

Ramsay Hunt Syndrome

The seventh pair of cranial nerves are called the facial nerves. They are composite nerves, which have both sensory and motor branches. Their sensory branches register sensations in the area of the ear, and also the sense of taste in the forward part of the tongue. Their motor branches control the muscles of facial expressions.

Shingles in one of the facial nerves is uncommon but not rare, and is likely to involve other nearby nerves as well, such as the pain-sensing trigeminal nerve, and the acoustic nerve, which registers sensations of hearing and balance in the inner ear. The result is known as Ramsay Hunt syndrome, and its typical symptoms include the following:

- Severe earache.

- Shingles rash on and near the ear, and in the ear canal.

- Loss of taste in part of the tongue.

- Paralysis of the facial muscles.

113

LIVING WITH SHINGLES

- Partial or complete loss of hearing.

- Inner ear disturbances, resulting in dizziness (vertigo) or nausea.

Some of these symptoms, such as the rash, ear pain, dizziness and nausea, and partial loss of taste are temporary, and pass with the acute infection. But the hearing loss and facial paralysis may linger for some time, and, in rare instances, may last indefinitely.

Like other forms of shingles, Ramsay-Hunt syndrome is treated with antiviral drugs, anti-inflammatory and narcotic analgesics, and sometimes corticosteroids. The anti-anxiety drug diazepam (Valium) may be prescribed to control dizziness. If facial paralysis persists after the acute stage, it can sometimes be relieved by surgically enlarging the channel where the nerve passes through the skull.

Scarring

A common but relatively less serious complication of shingles is imperfect healing of the affected skin. This is especially likely to occur when the skin is infected by bacteria as well as the virus. Instead of normal skin tissue, fibrous scar tissue forms. The scarred skin surface is abnormally smooth, and is often tight and slightly shiny. At first it may be discolored, but in time it usually turns a pale, silvery color. Furthermore, the area tends to lack some sensory nerve endings, so it may be at least partially numb.

Scarring is usually no more than a nuisance, but it can be unsightly or even disfiguring on the face. Sometimes the damage can be concealed with cosmetics or repaired by plastic surgery.

LIVING WITH SHINGLES

Recurrence

Usually if you have shingles once, you won't get it again for the rest of your life. But about one in twenty people who have shingles do suffer one or more later attacks. About half of these attacks recur in the same dermatome as before; the other half turn up elsewhere. Most affected individuals are severely immunosuppressed—their immune systems are greatly weakened by a disease such as AIDS, by drugs used to prevent rejection of an organ transplant, or by radiation or chemotherapy for cancer. Some are susceptible due to extreme old age. Recurrences are treated with the same techniques as those used for primary attacks.

Dissemination

Shingles is almost always confined to a single dermatome, or at most to two or three adjacent ones. Only in rare instances does the disease spread into other parts of the body, producing a rash elsewhere on the skin, or affecting other organs. Disseminated shingles is almost entirely confined to the severely immunosuppressed.

The spread of the virus to the internal organs of the body can be very dangerous. Two potential complications are likely to be especially serious: pneumonia, and encephalitis.

Pneumonia: When a person first catches chickenpox, the varicella-zoster virus spreads throughout the body, including the lungs. Children seldom suffer any ill-effects, but adolescents and adults, who tend to be more seriously affected by chickenpox, occasionally suffer inflammation of the lungs, or viral pneumonia. The same disorder sometimes follows disseminated shingles. Small air sacs of the lungs become inflamed and full of mucus and fluid, impairing the absorption of vital oxygen into the blood. In very severe instances, pneumonia can be life-threatening.

117

LIVING WITH SHINGLES

The main treatment for viral pneumonia is antiviral drugs, as it is for all forms of shingles. Anti-inflammatory analgesics are used to reduce pain and fever. Since there is a high risk for secondary infection by bacteria, antibiotics may be given to head it off.

Encephalitis: Encephalitis is an inflammation of the brain and its surrounding membranes. It is an uncommon disease, usually caused by some kind of viral infection. Like viral pneumonia, it is an occasional complication of both late-onset chickenpox and shingles.

When the virus inflames the brain and its membranes, it can cause direct damage to the cells. Moreover, when white blood cells of the immune system accumulate to fight the invaders, the tissues swell, and since there is no extra space within the skull for the swelling to expand into, pressure builds up, destroying brain cells or causing bleeding into the brain. The results may be brain damage or even death.

In the treatment of encephalitis, antiviral drugs are used to diminish the viral infection. Corticosteroids may be used to reduce inflammation and swelling. Anticonvulsant drugs may be needed to prevent or treat seizures. Anti-inflammatory analgesics may help relieve fever and pain.

118

Other Complications of Shingles

Connie Persig called her physician from the optometrist's office, and received immediate references to a dermatologist and an ophthalmologist. When they heard her symptoms suggested shingles near the eye, they both gave her appointments right away. The dermatologist started her on antiviral drugs that day. The opthalmologist performed a thorough examination, including measurement of the pressure within the eye, which might reveal glaucoma. He prescribed drops to relieve inflammation, and scheduled regular follow-up appointments.

For a few days, Connie felt even worse. The rash spread to her upper cheek and forehead, and the burning pain became more severe. The eyelids became swollen almost shut, and the eye itself became bloodshot and felt as if it had a cinder stuck in it. A combination of aspirin and codeine seemed to provide some relief, and helped her sleep. So did cool, wet compresses, anesthetic ointment, and anti-inflammatory eye-drops.

After a week, however, she began to notice a slight improvement, and then felt a little better every day. The opthalmologist reassured her that the infection apparently hadn't spread beyond the conjunctiva, and that there were no signs of glaucoma. The swelling of the eyelids subsided, and by three weeks most of the rash was crusted over.

By five weeks, the rash was healed over, leaving no evident scars. The pain continued for about three weeks longer, and then was interrupted by pain-free intervals that became progressively longer and more frequent. By three months, she was almost entirely recovered, but continued to suffer occa-

sional twinges, especially when she was tired or stressed. She returned periodically to be examined by the ophthalmologist, who had warned her that eye complications might crop up after her shingles disappeared. So far, though, she has had no problems.

Other Complications of Shingles

A Cause for Cautious Concern

You might find this account of the possible complications of shingles rather alarming. Please be reassured. First of all, the only really common complication is post-herpetic neuralgia, and, in most instances, even that painful condition resolves itself within a few weeks. Herpes zoster opthalmicus (HZO) is fairly common, but only a small minority of those affected suffer serious damage to the eye. Skin scarring is not uncommon, but usually not serious. Recurrence of shingles affects a relatively small proportion of those affected—about five percent.

Other potential complications range from uncommon to rare. Ramsay Hunt syndrome is very uncommon, and lasting facial paralysis or hearing loss even more so. Disseminated shingles occurs only among a small number of those whose immune systems are severely weakened, and pneumonia and encephalitis are rare even within that group.

Furthermore, many of the potential consequences—even the serious ones—can be successfully treated, so that the damage isn't permanent. And, finally, very, very few of these conditions are at all life-threatening.

121

LIVING WITH SHINGLES

It should be plain by now that the best way you can avoid such complications, or at least diminish their impact, is to obtain antiviral treatment promptly—just as soon as shingles is diagnosed. Complications are more likely to occur when the shingles attack itself is severe and long-lasting. Antiviral drugs greatly improve your chances of quick and easy recovery, but only if they are taken soon after the virus begins to reactivate. So if you have even vague symptoms that might signal the beginning of shingles (see Chapter 3), don't hesitate to seek professional help.

CHAPTER 6

Can Shingles Be Prevented?
The Varicella Vaccine

Catherine O'Fallon took her baby daughter to the pediatrician for a twelve-month checkup. "Now is the time," Dr. Gupta told her, "for Sheila to have her MMR immunization. That's for measles, mumps, and rubella. We recommend immunizing against chickenpox as well. It can be done at the same time."

"Chickenpox?" asked Mrs. O'Fallon. "Is it really worthwhile protecting against that?"

"Yes," replied Dr. Gupta, "we believe it really is."

"But I thought chickenpox was something children were supposed to catch, while they were young—so they wouldn't get it more seriously later on."

123

LIVING WITH SHINGLES

"That's what we used to think."

"And I thought it was particularly important for girls to get it over with, so they wouldn't come down with it during pregnancy."

"You're well informed," replied the doctor. "But now that we've found immunization gives long-lasting protection, our thinking has changed. You see, even small children sometimes have serious complications from chickenpox. It's better if they never get it at all. And there's another advantage as well."

"What's that?"

"Shingles. If Sheila's immune to chickenpox without ever having the disease, she may never have shingles."

The Prospect of Prevention

Never have shingles? A very attractive prospect. It may
not be a possibility for you, if you have already had
chickenpox—although ongoing research may change
that. But for children and others who have not yet
had chickenpox, there is now a very promising
method for preventing shingles: a vaccine that will
prevent them from getting chickenpox. If they don't
get chickenpox, then the varicella-zoster virus cannot
become stored in their nerve roots. No virus, no shingles—at least in theory.

Now, as we've said before, most adults *have* had
chickenpox—ninety-five percent by the time they are
eighteen. About four million people catch the disease
every year, and most of them are between the ages of
five and nine. Regardless of whether or not vaccination will eventually reduce shingles, there are sound
reasons for preventing chickenpox itself:

- Although chickenpox is considered mild,
  compared with some other rash diseases,
  it nonetheless makes many children quite
  miserable, and costs their families much
  time and inconvenience taking care of
  them.

125

- Not all individuals contract chickenpox during childhood. If they catch it as adolescents or adults, they are likely to be much sicker.

- Also likely to be more severely affected are those with weakened immune systems. Some have hereditary immunodeficiencies. Some have blood diseases such as leukemia or lymphoma. Some have AIDS. Some are being treated with corticosteroids, anticancer drugs, or radiation. These groups add up to a significant minority.

- Women who come down with chickenpox during pregnancy face a special risk. If they have the disease in early pregnancy, their babies may have serious birth defects. If they have it around the time of delivery, their babies may be severely infected.

- Perhaps most important, a small but meaningful number of those who get chickenpox don't recover promptly or completely. Up to nine thousand individuals are hospitalized each year for complications of this "mild" disease, and about one hundred die. The most common complication is secondary infection by bacteria, including a particularly nasty form of strep. Others include eye damage, pneumonia, and encephalitis, which are also potential complications of shingles (see chapter 5). Some individuals develop shingles itself, in a relatively short time, rather than many years later.

How the Vaccine Works

The varicella vaccine was first developed in the early 1970s by Japanese physician Michiaki Takahashi. The American pharmaceutical company Merck acquired rights to it in 1981, and for several years it was tested extensively (as all new vaccines must be) for safety and effectiveness. The Food and Drug Administration approved it in March 1995, and it has been commercially available ever since, under the brand name Varivax.

Vaccination is customarily offered to children from the time they are twelve months old. For those up to twelve years old, only a single shot is needed. Adolescents and adults are given two shots, spaced four weeks apart.

The vaccine is a live but weakened, or attenuated, form of the virus. It has been biologically manipulated so that it remains alive, but unable to reproduce well enough to cause disease. But it does retain enough of the features of the original virus for the vaccinated individual's immune system to recognize it and form antibodies to it. Thereafter, whenever the individual is exposed to the full-strength virus, the immune system will immediately react to it and keep it under control. In short, he or she will be immune to chickenpox.

Can Shingles Be Prevented?

The vaccine offers three main benefits:

- It completely prevents most chickenpox. It protects from seventy to ninety percent of those vaccinated against any symptomatic disease, and ninety-five percent against severe disease.

- When vaccinated individuals do experience a "breakthrough" infection, it is much milder than usual. The fever is lower, the number of bumps is much smaller, and recovery is quicker.

- It appears to offer almost complete protection against complications of chickenpox, probably by reducing the impact of the virus itself.

The vaccine also shows promise in protecting unvaccinated individuals who are exposed to chickenpox, if it is administered within three days of the exposure.

The vaccine itself is not known to cause any serious health problems, and its negative side effects are relatively few, minor, and temporary. The most common is inflammation at the injection site, with the typical symptoms of swelling, redness, and soreness. A low fever and a mild headache are also relatively common. Much rarer is an outbreak of rash, which may represent a low-level infection, and may be contagious. As you might expect, side effects are likely to be more severe among those individuals at risk for severe infection—older individuals, and others with weak immune systems.

The Vaccine Controversy

Despite the apparent benefits of immunization, many doctors have until quite recently been hesitant to give the vaccine to their clients. Their main reservation is simple: they are not sure the protection will last.

Infection with the varicella virus itself provides lifelong immunity to chickenpox. But will immunity provided by the weakened virus of the vaccine give equally long-lasting protection? If it doesn't, vaccinated individuals might end up worse off than ever. That is, instead of catching chickenpox during childhood, they might come down with it later in life, when it is likely to be more severe, and more likely to be followed by dangerous complications.

At present, there can be no absolute answer to this argument. As is true of all new vaccines, the full extent of protection offered by the varicella vaccine won't be known for decades. But with every passing year, there is additional evidence that immunity does *not* wane with time. In this country, the vaccine has been clinically tested for more than ten years. In Japan, the period is more than twenty years. In these tests, immunity has been demonstrated to persist, and neither the risk nor the severity of disease has shown any statistical increase with the passage of time.

131

LIVING WITH SHINGLES

Moreover, testing for antibodies to the virus is a fairly simple and reliable process, so it isn't difficult to determine whether or not a vaccinated individual is still immune. It may prove advisable in the future to perform such follow-up tests periodically, and to provide booster shots to individuals whose immunity is waning.

In any event, more and more health professionals are now weighing in to support routine immunization—especially of children. Vaccination is recommended by such key organizations and institutions as the American Academy of Pediatrics, the American Academy of Family Practitioners, and the Centers for Disease Control and Prevention. The Centers for Disease Control and Prevention have also added the varicella vaccine to the Vaccines for Children program, which supplies free doses to children whose families couldn't otherwise afford them.

An editorial by Eugene D. Shapiro and Philip S. LaRussa in the *Journal of the American Medical Association* sums up the sentiments of most experts concerning vaccination: "Just do it!"

Current Recommendations for Immunization

Vaccination is now recommended for most people who haven't already had chickenpox. These include all children between the ages of one and twelve, with limited exceptions. They also include certain groups of adolescents and adults, such as the following:

- Teachers, day-care workers, and others who are regularly in close contact with children.

- Health-care workers who are in regular contact with the sick.

- Uninfected family members of individuals with chickenpox.

- Individuals who live in close contact with one another, such as college students and prison inmates.

- Women of child-bearing age, regardless of whether or not they

133

have immediate plans to conceive. Vaccination should not be performed during pregnancy.

- Travelers to foreign countries.

We mentioned exceptions. The following groups are "contraindicated" (to use the medical jargon) for vaccination:

- Individuals suffering from an active, severe infectious illness, such as tuberculosis.

- Individuals who are allergic to components of the vaccine, such as gelatin and the antibiotic neomycin.

- Individuals who have within recent months received blood transfusions, or injections of blood products such as immune globulins.

- Pregnant women. The vaccine hasn't been proved harmless to developing fetuses. At the same time, there is no evidence that it has caused any damage when administered accidentally during pregnancy.

134

Can Shingles Be Prevented?

- Individuals with weakened immune systems, from diseases such as lymphoma or AIDS, or from corticosteroids, or from drugs used to prevent transplant rejection or to kill cancer cells.

This last category may seem ironic. It would appear that those who need protection most are restrained from getting it. The reason is simply caution. If an individual has a very weak immune system, the vaccine may be unable to stimulate it sufficiently to achieve immunity to the virus. Instead, it may make the person even more susceptible to infection.

Research is being carried out to determine just what the effects of the vaccine might be upon those who suffer from various kinds of immune deficiency. One of the first groups to be tested has been children with leukemia, who are at special risk for severe chickenpox and dangerous complications. The results are promising: After vaccination, fewer of these children get chickenpox, and the consequences are less serious if they do. Approval of the vaccine has been extended to such children, as long as the disease is in a relatively quiet phase.

But Will It Stop Shingles?

Public health authorities hope that varicella vaccination will become virtually universal, just as smallpox vaccination is. If it does, then chickenpox will eventually disappear, as smallpox has. And if chickenpox disappears, shingles should gradually disappear as well.

There is at least some evidence that vaccinated individuals will not only escape getting chickenpox, but also escape getting shingles later on. We mentioned the example of children with leukemia. Without vaccination, many of them suffer severely from chickenpox, and then develop shingles just a few years later. After being vaccinated, the rates of both chickenpox and shingles are greatly reduced. Whether this reduction will also occur in adults, who ordinarily don't get shingles until many years after having chickenpox, isn't yet known. But the evidence seems promising.

These prospects, cheery as they may be for future generations, probably offer little or no comfort to you who are reading this book. Almost certainly, you have already had chickenpox. If you haven't already had shingles, you run an increasing risk of getting it with every year you live. And even if you have already had

Can Shingles Be Prevented?

shingles once, there is at least a slight chance that you will get it again. So, you might well ask, what can the varicella vaccine do for *me*?

The short-form answer is: nobody knows for sure. But the full answer is somewhat more positive. For there is at least partial evidence that varicella vaccine may not only prevent shingles indirectly, by preventing chickenpox, but also directly, when given later in life.

As we've explained earlier, shingles seems to be triggered by declining immunity to the varicella-zoster virus. Either the immune system no longer recognizes the virus as a foreign invader, or is no longer able to attack it effectively—or both. But a limited experiment has been performed that involved vaccinating about two hundred older people and then measuring their levels of immune antibodies to the virus over a period of four years. The levels not only rose right after vaccination, as might be expected, but remained fairly high in most subjects for the duration of the study. Furthermore, very few of the subjects developed shingles, and all the cases were mild.

Much larger studies are now under way, here and in Finland, which should further clarify the possible effects of the vaccine on shingles. Both studies involve many thousands of subjects, aged fifty-five or over, who have already had chickenpox. Half the subjects in each study are being given the vaccine; the other half are not. After several years, researchers will compare the rates of shingles in each group, to see whether the subjects who got vaccinated have lower rates than those who did not.

Such tests are of necessity fairly elaborate. They must have large numbers of subjects, and the division between those receiving the vaccine and those who are controls must be as random as possible. Moreover, the studies must be double-blinded. That is, all subjects receive either a shot of the vaccine or a lookalike "dummy" shot, and neither the researchers nor the recipients know which is which.

These tests will take time to produce results. Even five years may not be enough for any statistically meaningful differences in shingles rates to appear. The subjects may have to be followed ten years or more, and in the end the results may not be conclusive.

The first review will probably not take place until the first years of the new century. Meanwhile, the limited evidence we do have is at least promising. So, here's hoping that the new vaccine will prove to be an effective weapon against an old plague.

Questions and Answers about Shingles

Shingles Basics

If I come down with shingles, what kinds of symptoms can I expect?

There are two main symptoms. One is a patchy rash of small bumps that turn into blisters. The other is burning or stabbing pain in the area of the rash. It may begin before the rash appears, and may persist after the rash has healed.

LIVING WITH SHINGLES

Is it true that shingles only turns up on certain parts of the body?

Shingles can occur just about anywhere on the body. But it occurs most frequently on the trunk, especially near the waist (the name shingles comes from a word meaning "belt"). The second most common location is the face, especially the region of the forehead, eye, and nose.

When I had shingles, the rash was just a narrow band that ran from my breastbone around to my spine, on one side. Why did it appear in just that area?

Shingles is caused by inflammation of one or more sensory nerves (usually just one, or even a single branch of one) by the same virus that causes chickenpox. The sensory nerves are located in pairs along the spinal column, and each nerve of the pair serves a limited area on one side of the body. After a chickenpox infection, the virus survives, alive but inactive, in the root of the nerve, near the point of attachment to the spinal cord. When the virus reactivates, reproducing and spreading through the nerve, it produces pain and a skin rash in the specific area, or dermatome, served by the nerve. When you had shingles, it appeared in a single dermatome on your trunk.

140

Questions and Answers about Shingles

I had chickenpox many years ago. I'm now in my sixties, and haven't had shingles, but I'm told that the older I get, the greater chance I have of getting it. Is that so?

As you get older, your immune system—your body's ability to recognize and defend itself from infection—becomes steadily weaker. Shingles apparently results when the immune system is no longer strong enough to prevent reactivation of the chickenpox vaccine in a nerve root. So, the older you get, the greater is your risk of shingles.

My thirty-eight-year-old niece just came down with shingles. Isn't that unusual?

Shingles in younger people is uncommon, but it happens. Those most likely to get shingles are the immunosuppressed—people who lack the protection of a normal immune system. They include the following:

- Those who are taking drugs (chemotherapy) or receiving radiation for cancer. These treatments are intended to kill cancer cells, but they kill cells of the immune system as well.

141

- Those taking drugs intentionally designed to suppress the immune system, so as to prevent tissue rejection after an organ transplant.

- Those taking anti-inflammatory cortico-steroids for diseases such as lupus or arthritis. These drugs weaken the immune system.

- Those who have blood diseases such as leukemia, lymphoma, or Hodgkin's dis-ease, which naturally weaken the immune system.

- Those infected with HIV, the human immunovirus that attacks the immune system and causes AIDS.

In addition, for some individuals, younger or older, shingles is apparently triggered when the immune system is temporarily weakened by some acute disease, or by severe stress. And some come down with it for no apparent reason—"out of the blue."

Questions and Answers about Shingles

If shingles is caused by the chickenpox virus, why would I get shingles rather than chickenpox later in life?

Apparently, once you have had chickenpox, your immunity to it remains strong enough to prevent another outbreak. But your immune system may not remain strong enough to prevent the reactivation of the virus that is hiding in a nerve root. That reactivated virus, confined within the nerve, is what causes shingles.

Does the shingles rash look like chickenpox?

Both the chickenpox and shingles rashes are made up of small bumps that turn into blisters. But the chickenpox rash is scattered over much of the body, while the shingles rash is usually limited to the area of a single dermatome. The shingles rash is also more concentrated, and the pain accompanying it is more severe than the itching of chickenpox.

How do I know if I have shingles?

About the only way you or your doctor can be sure you have shingles is to identify the rash when it appears. Symptoms that occur before that are often too vague or too easily mistaken for something else to make diagnosis certain.

However, you might consult your doctor if you experience a couple of telltale signs of the disease, other than rash. The main one is tingling, itching, or pain in a limited area on one side of your body or face. The pain also tends to be distinctive: sharp, stabbing, or burning, and relieved somewhat by rest. And, of course, if you see any signs of rash, you should get in touch with your doctor immediately.

Is rash ever the first symptom of shingles?

Usually the rash appears only after other symptoms—even if the earlier symptoms are too vague to identify. The reactivation of the virus takes place in the nerve root, and it takes time—usually a couple of days—for the infection to move through the nerve fiber to the skin, where it produces the rash.

What is the usual course of the shingles rash?

The rash appears in successive, overlapping "crops." Each crop goes through four stages:

- *Papules:* small bumps on a reddish base.

144

Questions and Answers about Shingles

- *Vesicles:* blisters, filled with clear lymph fluid.

- *Pustules:* enlarged blisters, filled with pus—lymph fluid, white blood cells, and cell fragments.

- *Scabs:* dry, crusted remains of pustules after they have broken open.

How long can I expect the shingles rash to last?

The rash usually lasts about a week to ten days from the time it first appears to the time that most of its scabs are crusted over. Complete healing may take a week or two longer.

Will the pain go away when the rash disappears?

Episodes of pain are likely to occur for another couple of weeks after the skin is healed. The normal duration of shingles is up to five weeks. If the pain persists or comes back after that, it is described as post-herpetic neuralgia.

145

LIVING WITH SHINGLES

If I get shingles, will it make me so sick that I have to go to bed?

Shingles varies widely in its severity. It may be so mild that it is hardly noticeable, or so severe that you are completely incapacitated. Even if you are able to continue your ordinary activities, you may find that the pain is relieved by getting extra rest.

What are my chances of recovering completely from shingles?

Most people do recover completely, without any complications. Those seriously affected may suffer persistent pain—what's called post-herpetic neuralgia. Other possible complications are less common.

My wife had a terrible case of shingles last year. Is it at all likely that she'll get it again?

It is uncommon for anyone to have shingles more than once. The overall risk is about one in twenty, but most of those are people with extremely weak immune systems, as the result of other disease, medical treatment, or advanced old age.

The Varicella-Zoster Virus

When I had shingles, my doctor said it was caused by the varicella-zoster virus. What has that got to do with chickenpox?

The varicella-zoster virus, or VZV for short, causes both chickenpox and shingles. *Varicella* is the medical name for chickenpox; *zoster*, the medical name for shingles.

When my husband had shingles, I discouraged my eighty-nine-year-old mother from visiting us, for fear she might catch it. Was I wrong to be concerned?

When you have shingles, you can't give shingles to anyone else. You can give chickenpox to someone who hasn't already had it, but the chances are that your mother has already had chickenpox.

LIVING WITH SHINGLES

My daughter, who works, has asked me to babysit with my seven-year old grandson while he's home with chickenpox. I know that I'm immune to chickenpox, since I had it myself years ago. But can I catch shingles from my grandson?

It is generally agreed that you can't catch shingles from someone with chickenpox. If you get shingles, the virus is your own, left over from the chickenpox you once had.

I get confused about germs. What's the difference between viruses and bacteria?

Bacteria are complete, living cells—like the cells in your body. Each cell has a nucleus, containing chain-like molecules of DNA that carry the genetic code for reproduction. Bacteria can reproduce and multiply on their own.

The particles of a virus are much smaller and simpler. Each virus particle has two basic parts. One is a single length of either DNA or a similar molecule called RNA. The other is a coating of protein. Viruses cannot reproduce on their own. Virus particles must invade living cells and take over their reproductive machinery, so they will produce more virus. The new virus particles can then migrate from the host cells to invade other cells, spreading the infection.

148

Questions and Answers about Shingles

In practical terms, the main difference between bacterial and viral infections is the way they are treated. Bacterial infections are treated with antibiotics, which kill bacterial cells. Antibiotics are ineffective against viruses. Viral diseases are treated with antiviral drugs, which hinder reproduction of the virus. Also, many viral diseases can be prevented with vaccines, which strengthen the immune system against specific viruses.

My doctor tells me that the chickenpox virus is related to the viruses that cause cold sores and genital herpes. How is that?

VZV is one of the herpesviruses. Other viruses in this group cause cold sores, genital herpes, and mononucleosis. They have several traits in common. They only reproduce in human cells. They are extremely contagious. They never completely die out in their human hosts, although their effects may be controlled by the hosts' immune systems.

How does the immune system work?

Your immune system is made up of different kinds of white blood cells, plus certain chemicals they produce. It has two basic mechanisms. It attacks any sub-

149

stances in your body that have been identified as foreign, and either destroys them or makes them inactive. It also learns to recognize many specific foreign substances the first time they enter your body, so they can be attacked even faster and more effectively if they ever appear again.

How is it that I became immune to chickenpox, but only after I had the disease?

When you were first infected by the chickenpox virus (probably when you were a child) your immune system didn't recognize it, and was relatively slow in mounting a counterattack against it. So you had to suffer chickenpox for a few days, until your immune system got control of it.

In the process, your immune system did learn to recognize the virus. Whenever you were exposed to it again, your immune system attacked it immediately and effectively, so you've never again had chickenpox.

Why do most people catch chickenpox in childhood, rather than later on?

The virus is extremely contagious. Its particles are easily passed on, mainly in small droplets of moisture that

150

are breathed out by the infected person, starting even before any obvious symptoms appear. When one child in a household, a day-care center, or a classroom gets chickenpox, it becomes very likely that others will catch it as well. So by such exposures, most children end up getting chickenpox before they are adolescents.

When I had shingles, I was so sick I had to go to the hospital for a few days. One of the nurses had never had chickenpox, and was not permitted to care for me. Why was that?

For children, chickenpox is usually (though not always) a mild disease. But individuals who don't catch it until they are adolescents or adults are likely to suffer more severe attacks, and are at greater risk for dangerous complications. When you had shingles, your blisters contained particles of virus, and you could have given chickenpox to the nurse who had never had it. So she was told to avoid contact with you.

Is it true that even though I am immune to chickenpox, there's still some of the virus in my body?

The varicella-zoster virus, like other herpesviruses, never completely dies out in the body. Your immune system prevents it from causing chickenpox ever again. But the virus "hides out" in the roots of sensory nerves, and may eventually cause shingles.

For years I've suffered from recurrent cold sores on my upper lip. I understand that they are caused by a virus that is related to the virus for chickenpox and shingles. Why is it that cold sores keep coming back, but chickenpox and shingles occur just once each?

Herpes simplex type one, which causes cold sores, is less well controlled by the immune system than is the varicella-zoster virus, following a first infection. So cold sores keep coming back periodically, although later attacks tend to be less serious than the first one.

The immune system usually provides permanent immunity to chickenpox. But it may not remain able to prevent the virus in the nerve roots from reactivating and causing shingles. But shingles itself seems to restore the ability of the immune system to recognize and attack the virus, so that a repeat attack is rare.

My sister-in-law has never had chickenpox. When she was pregnant a few years ago, they gave her immunoglobulins so she wouldn't get infected dur-

ing that period. Could immunoglobulins also head off shingles?

Immunoglobulins, also known as antibodies, are chemicals naturally produced by the immune system to match specific invaders, such as viruses. Whenever an antibody meets the matching virus, it becomes attached to the virus particle, marking it for destruction.

A concentrate of antibodies to the varicella-zoster virus, called varicella-zoster immune globulin (VZIG), is often injected into individuals such as pregnant women, who need extra protection against the virus. (Chickenpox contracted during pregnancy can cause birth defects.)

VZIG has also been tried as a protection against shingles, but it isn't effective for that purpose.

Shingles Treatment

When my father had shingles, friends recommended all sorts of folk remedies for it. What are now considered the most effective forms of treatment?

Only in recent times has much been known about shingles and its causes. Before that, a lot of different remedies were tried, and most of them didn't work. Now there are two main forms of treatment:

- *Antiviral drugs*, which directly attack the virus that causes the disease.

- *Palliative remedies*, which relieve the symptoms of the disease even if they don't affect its course. These include painkillers of various kinds, and techniques to reduce psychological stress.

154

Questions and Answers about Shingles

I've heard that if I get shingles, I should seek treatment right away. Aside from making me more comfortable, why is that so important?

The first line of defense against shingles is antiviral drugs, and they must be taken early in the course of the disease to be fully effective.

How do antiviral drugs work? Do they kill the virus?

Antiviral drugs don't kill the virus the way that antibiotics kill bacteria. Instead, they stop it from reproducing, so it does less harm. They change the form of the DNA molecule of the virus so that it can't completely copy itself. But the existing virus survives, until the immune system eventually gets control of it. So the earlier treatment with antiviral drugs starts, the less virus accumulates in the nerve. The disease won't last as long, and its symptoms are likely to be less severe.

My neighbor said that when she had shingles, she didn't even call her doctor because the rash hardly bothered her. Was that wise?

She was taking a chance that the attack would soon resolve itself without treatment. Antiviral drugs, which must be prescribed by a doctor, are now rec-

155

ommended for anyone who has shingles, even if the attack is mild.

What are the antiviral drugs most widely used for shingles?

There are three antiviral drugs commonly used for shingles. The oldest is acyclovir, which is taken both by injection (intravenously) and by mouth. The brand name of the pill form is Zovirax. The other two, taken only by mouth, are famcyclovir (trade name Famvir) and valacyclovir (Valtrex).

If I take an antiviral drug, do I have to worry about serious side effects?

Antiviral drugs act selectively upon the virus, and have little or no effect on normal cells. Their side effects are usually no more than mildly annoying. The most common are headache and digestive-tract irritations—nausea, and either constipation or diarrhea. Less common is irritation of the kidneys. You should, of course, report any side effects to your doctor, but they are seldom troublesome enough to make you stop taking the drug.

Questions and Answers about Shingles

What drugs can I take to relieve the pain of shingles?

There are essentially four types of painkillers used to make shingles pain more tolerable:

- Aspirin, ibuprofen, and other non-steroidal anti-inflammatory drugs (NSAIDs for short).

- Acetominophen, of which the best known form is Tylenol.

- Narcotics, also known as opioids.

- Corticosteroids, sometimes called simply steroids.

I get confused by all the different painkillers sold over the counter. For instance, what's the difference between aspirin and ibuprofen?

Aspirin and ibuprofen differ slightly in their chemical composition, but they work in similar ways. They are the only over-the-counter drugs in a group called nonsteroidal anti-inflammatory drugs, or NSAIDS. That is, they relieve inflammation, but they aren't steroids. They also seem to affect the perception of pain in the central nervous system.

LIVING WITH SHINGLES

Aspirin and ibuprofen seem to upset my stomach, and my doctor recommends Tylenol or Datril instead. Do they work differently from aspirin and ibuprofen?

Among the possible side effects of NSAIDs is irritation of the stomach lining, sometimes to the extent of causing ulcers and bleeding. Tylenol and Datril are forms of acetaminophen, which affects only the central perception of pain. Acetaminophen doesn't relieve inflammation, but it doesn't irritate the stomach, either.

Incidentally, some over-the-counter formulations, such as Excedrin, contain both acetaminophen and aspirin.

My shingles pain was so bad my doctor recommended a narcotic, but I was scared of becoming addicted, so I wouldn't take it. Was I right?

Narcotics are among the most effective painkillers known. They are also called opioids because they are either derived from opium or chemically similar to it. Taken in large amounts in order to get high, they can lead to dependence and even addiction. But taken in moderate amounts, under medical supervision, to relieve physical pain, they seldom if ever cause such problems.

158

Also, opioids vary a lot in their potency. Those prescribed for shingles are usually mild varieties, such as codeine or propoxyphene (brand name Darvon).

I heard that steroids are really good at relieving inflammation. But my doctor didn't want me to take them. Why?

Steroids, more accurately called corticosteroids, are indeed very effective in relieving inflammation. But they have many undesirable side effects, including a tendency to suppress your immune system. Even while they are relieving the symptoms of shingles, they may be reinforcing one of its underlying causes. Many doctors don't feel that the benefits of the drugs outweigh the drawbacks, except in special circumstances.

Are the steroids used to fight inflammation the same as those that athletes take to bulk themselves up?

The term steroid is confusing. As popularly used, it refers both to the corticosteroid drugs used to relieve inflammation, and to the anabolic steroids used (and abused) to improve athletic performance. The two have nothing in common.

LIVING WITH SHINGLES

When my sister had shingles, her dermatologist gave her some stuff to dilute with water and apply as a wet compress. It seemed to give her some relief. What was it?

Aluminum acetate, also known as Burow's solution, has long been used to relieve skin irritations. It is an astringent, which firms and dries the skin, and apparently helps draw out some of the irritants that trigger pain.

I've heard that shingles is sometimes more itchy than painful. What sort of treatment is given for that?

Topical anti-itch medications (known formally as antiprurients) are used to relieve the intense itching that shingles sometimes causes. One that you are doubtless familiar with is calamine lotion. Others are doxepin (Zonalon) and tolamine salicylate (Aspercreme).

Questions and Answers about Shingles

When my aunt had shingles, her doctor suggested that she crush some aspirin tablets into powder, mix it with rubbing alcohol, and dab it on the rash. It really seemed to help. Is this a common remedy?

Nobody has made a commercial formulation of crushed aspirin and evaporating fluid, but a number of clinical experiments have found that it relieves shingles pain at least temporarily as the fluid dries.

Would the kind of ointment used for insect bites and burns give any relief from shingles?

A common type of ointment for skin irritation has a topical anesthetic, such as lidocaine, prilocaine, or pramoxine, as its active ingredient. It doesn't just suppress pain—it makes the skin numb—but it can provide very welcome temporary relief.

When my neighbor had shingles, she started doing some exercises to reduce psychological stress. What has shingles got to do with stress?

Pain of many kinds can be be triggered or intensified by psychological stress. Conversely, the reduction of stress can actually relieve the perception of pain. Stress-reducing techniques can powerfully reinforce

LIVING WITH SHINGLES

the effects of drugs and other medical agents in relieving shingles pain.

I have long used a technique called progressive relaxation to help me get to sleep. I concentrate on specific muscle groups in my body, from my feet to my forehead, and imagine them as comfortable and relaxed. I've heard that the same technique can be used to help cope with pain. Is that so?

One of the best ways to control psychological stress is by achieving physical relaxation. Many psychologists believe that it is impossible to be both physically relaxed and psychologically tense at the same time. To be effective, relaxation exercises have to be practiced regularly until they become habitual.

A friend of mine at work says that meditation helped him a lot when he got shingles. How does it work?

Meditation is an ancient technique of mental distraction. Its traditional function is to separate the mind from the limits of ordinary reality, and to achieve inner peace. But it can also reduce stress and pain by distracting your attention away from them. It is per-

162

formed by sitting or lying in a relaxed position, repeating a single word over and over, and allowing your mind to become as empty and passive as possible.

I've heard that mental techniques called directed imagery and sensory substitution are used to relieve shingles pain. What are they?

Both are techniques that use the power of imagination to divert attention from pain or to reshape the perception of it. Guided imagery involves forming a mental image of a pleasant, tranquil scene and then immersing yourself entirely in it, until you are free of stress and the consciousness of pain. Sensory substitution is imagining that a painful sensation has been replaced with some other, nonpainful one, such as coolness or mild prickling. Like other methods of stress control, these techniques can only be mastered through concentration and repeated practice.

When the pain of shingles on my chest kept me from sleeping, my doctor recommended wrapping the area with an elastic sports bandage. It really did help—but how did it work?

What your doctor recommended was a simple application of a natural process of pain relief called coun-

terirritation. The mildly irritating sensations produced by the pressure of the elastic bandage are
transmitted to the central nervous system, where they
trigger reactions that diminish the perception of
pain. Another form of counterirritation that sometimes helps with shingles is a liniment such as oil of
wintergreen, which initially makes the skin tingle.

**When my cousin had shingles, she was given some-
thing called a TENS unit to help relieve her pain. It
used electricity in some way. What was it?**

Transcutaneous electrical nerve stimulation, or
TENS for short, is most often used to treat joint and
muscle pain, but it is also occasionally used to relieve
shingles. A portable machine produces mild pulses of
electrical current, which pass through electrodes to
the skin, provoking a tingling sensation. It is thought
to relieve pain through the process of counterirritation.

Post-Herpetic Neuralgia

After suffering miserably from shingles, I thought the pain would go away not long after the rash disappeared. Instead, I'm still in lots of pain. What's the matter?

Unfortunately, you have what is called post-herpetic neuralgia—PHN for short. It is the most common complication of shingles, and it is defined as significant pain that persists or returns more than five weeks after the first appearance of the shingles rash.

I'm just getting over shingles. A friend of mine who had it six months ago is still in serious pain. What are my chances of going through the same thing?

Nobody can predict exactly who will get PHN after shingles. But certain factors seem to raise the risk:

- *Severe shingles.* If you have a severe attack of shingles, and especially if you suffered significant pain before the rash appeared, you are more likely to get PHN.

165

- *Increasing age.* The older you are when you have shingles, the more likely you are to suffer PHN afterward.

- *Extreme immunosuppression.* Individuals with greatly weakened immune systems, from disease or medical treatment, are more likely to suffer PHN after shingles.

If I do get PHN after I recover from shingles, how long will it last and how much will I suffer?

PHN, like shingles itself, varies enormously. For some, it is no more than a minor annoyance; for others, it is a disabling misery. Most people get over it within a few weeks or months; for an unfortunate minority, the pain may continue indefinitely.

I was told that once the shingles rash heals, the virus is no longer active. So, why does the pain persist?

Apparently, the acute attack of the virus causes lasting damage to nerve cells, and this damage in turn causes pain sensations even after the virus has become inactive.

Is it possible to get PHN without having shingles first?

PHN is a direct consequence of shingles. It doesn't occur on its own.

Mostly, the pain I have now is the same as when I had shingles. But there's also something new. The lightest touch—just wearing a shirt—can set off awful stabs of pain. What's going on?

The mysterious and very distressing symptom called allodynia is more typical of PHN than of shingles. Allodynia is pain triggered by some sensation that is not in itself painful—such as a light, moving touch across the skin. Apparently the harmless sensation, transmitted through nerves that don't normally sense pain, somehow trigger the nerves that do transmit pain sensations.

LIVING WITH SHINGLES

This continuing pain really wears me down. I get very little sleep. I've lost my appetite. I don't want to go anywhere or see anybody. Is this common?

Even more than shingles, PHN can be physically and emotionally debilitating. Insomnia, loss of appetite, depression, and social withdrawal are indeed common. Fortunately, there are many forms of treatment, both physical and mental, now available to help you manage these consequences of pain.

I took an antiviral drug when I first came down with shingles, but my doctor says it won't work against PHN. Is that so?

Antiviral drugs are only helpful at an early stage of shingles, when they prevent the virus from reproducing further. PHN occurs after the virus has become inactive, so antivirals have no effect on it.

My doctor tells me that the aspirin and codeine I took when I had shingles won't be as helpful now I have PHN. Is she right?

The painkillers commonly used to relieve the pain of shingles—aspirin and other nonsteroidal anti-inflammatory drugs (NSAIDs), acetominophen (Tylenol),

168

and narcotics such as codeine—are for some reason less effective against PHN.

I've heard that the pain that follows shingles is now often treated with antidepressant drugs. Is that because the pain causes depression?

Just as antiviral drugs have become leading tools in relieving shingles, so antidepressants have become leading tools in relieving PHN. Specific antidepressants known as tricyclics are used to treat PHN, but they are given in much smaller doses than those used to treat depression. They apparently work by hindering the transmission of pain impulses to the brain.

If I take an antidepressant for PHN, what side affects do I have to worry about?

The side effects of antidepressants, especially when taken in small doses, are usually no more than mildly annoying. Probably the most common is dryness of the mouth, and the next most common is constipation. Other possible nuisances include "cold" sweating, drowsiness, susceptibility to fainting, heart palpitations, and weight gain from increased appetite.

LIVING WITH SHINGLES

Is it true that drugs used for epileptic seizures are also used for PHN?

Anticonvulsant drugs are used to control the abnormal activity in brain cells that produces the convulsions of epilepsy. They are also sometimes useful in controlling spasms of stabbing pain in PHN, especially those triggered by nonpainful sensations (allodynia).

What was the special ointment my aunt was given for the pain she had after shingles? It burned like the dickens when she first put it on, but after awhile she got used to it, and it did give her some relief.

A topical ointment sometimes used for PHN is based on capsaicin—the active ingredient in hot peppers. Capsaicin is thought to lower the level of a chemical that enhances the transmission of pain impulses to the central nervous system. When first applied to the skin, it produces a burning, stinging sensation, which is followed by at least some reduction in sensitivity to pain.

Questions and Answers about Shingles

A friend of mine says he found biofeedback helpful in controlling the pain he had following shingles. How does it work?

Relaxation helps to relieve pain by reducing stress. Biofeedback might be described as mechanically assisted relaxation. It is a machine that registers physical signs of stress and makes them audible or visible. The higher the level of stress, the stronger the output. Apparently, when you become more aware of your level of stress, you are better able to control it, and to achieve relaxation.

Hypnosis is sometimes used to treat painful conditions like chronic headaches. Might it help relieve PHN?

Hypnosis is occasionally used in efforts to relieve stubborn PHN. In a hypnotic trance you become strongly susceptible to suggestion, which can greatly alter your perception—including the perception of pain. Hypnotic suggestion can make a part of your body numb, or make a painful sensation feel like some other, nonpainful one (sensory substitution). The effects may persist after you emerge from the trance—a phenomenon called posthypnotic suggestion. The big drawback to hypnosis is that many people are not capable of being hypnotized.

LIVING WITH SHINGLES

A friend of mine at work has been on disability for months for the pain he's suffered ever since he had shingles. Recently he's been advised to get psychotherapy. Would that really help with his pain?

Such forms of psychotherapy as cognitive therapy and behavioral therapy are sometimes helpful in relieving persistent PHN. Psychotherapy may not directly relieve pain, but may help keep it from intensifying, in the downward spiral of what's called a "pain cycle," in which pain leads to stress, which leads to more pain, and so forth. Just as important, therapy can help patients cope better with pain, so that it doesn't become completely disabling.

I've heard that something called a nerve block can stop pain sensation completely. Would that be helpful with PHN?

Nerve blocks completely stop the transmission of impulses. They are sometimes used to treat PHN, usually as a last resort, when the pain is severe and long-lasting, and other approaches have failed. They have many potentially serious side effects, and even the most radical of them—completely severing the nerves—offers only temporary relief.

Questions and Answers about Shingles

My sister has a very capable doctor, but so far the things he's done for the pain she's had since getting shingles aren't much help. Now he's suggesting she try the pain clinic at the university medical center. What's the advantage of that?

Pain clinics, often associated with a teaching hospital or university medical school, use a team of experts that might include a neurologist, an anesthesiologist, a physical therapist, and a psychologist, among others. The team prepares a systematic treatment plan, often involving several different forms of treatment at once. The goals are not only to reduce pain and speed recovery, but also to restore normal function. The combination of physical and psychological approaches can help patients cope with their condition and carry on with their lives, even if they haven't completely recovered.

I think I'm beginning to feel a little better. What will my recovery from PHN be like?

Attacks of pain will alternate with periods of relief, and the attacks will gradually become shorter and less intense, while the pain-free periods become longer. The process may extend for months, but once the pattern becomes established, you can at least be reassured that eventual recovery is on the way.

Other Complications of Shingles

I thought shingles appeared mainly around the middle of the body, but my father-in-law has it on his upper face. Is that common?

Shingles does occur most often in various parts of the trunk, especially the dermatomes close to the waist. But the dermatome of the upper face, from the forehead to the end of the nose, is the most common single site of the disease, accounting for about fifteen percent of all cases.

I've just been to my doctor for a bad headache on one side of my head. I thought it might be migraine. He got all concerned when he spotted a little patch of rash near the tip of my nose, and wants me to see an ophthalmologist. What's the problem?

A patch of rash near the tip of the nose, called Hutchinson's sign, is considered early evidence of shingles originating in the upper, or ophthalmic, branch of the trigeminal nerve in the face. This form of shingles is called herpes zoster ophthalmicus, or

174

Questions and Answers about Shingles

HZO for short. Its particular danger is that the virus infection may spread to the eye, so it is advisable to have an ophthalmologist as part of the treatment team.

When my brother first showed signs of shingles near his eye, his doctor started treatment that very day. What kind of harm can shingles do to the eye?

HZO is considered especially dangerous because the eye is a delicate organ, and quite susceptible to damage. The viral infection can affect just about any part of the eye, and the damage it causes may be irreversible. It may even eventually cause the diminishment or complete loss of a crucial function—vision. That's why prompt treatment of HZO is so crucial.

Herpes near the eye is sure unsightly. My sister-in-law's eyelids—especially the upper one—are swollen almost shut, as if she'd been slugged in the eye. She refuses to go out—can't bear to be seen. Will all this go away?

Inflammation of the eyelids is a very common consequence of HZO, and it usually subsides when the acute attack ends. But severe inflammation may permanently damage the lids, so that some of the lashes are lost, or the lids don't close properly.

LIVING WITH SHINGLES

Shingles has given my uncle a bad case of pinkeye. It hurts him a lot. Will it do any permanent harm?

The virus often inflames the conjunctiva, a transparent membrane over the white of the eye, or the sclera, the white of the eye, and the other outer layers of the eyeball. The inflammation may be very painful, but usually subsides without causing permanent damage.

When an ophthalmologist examined my eye after I came down with shingles, she said that she was looking for signs of keratitis. What's that?

Keratitis is an inflammation of the cornea, a kind of transparent window in the front of the eye. Keratitis is a common complication of HZO, and it can lead either directly or by secondary bacterial infection to permanent ulceration or scarring that harms vision.

I've heard that shingles of the eye can cause glaucoma, and I know that glaucoma can cause blindness. Is this a serious risk?

Glaucoma is caused by abnormally high pressure of the fluids in the eyeball. The pressure can gradually damage the optic nerve, leading to "tunnel" vision,

176

or, in extreme cases, blindness. The inflammation of HZO can sometimes lead to an increase in this inter-ocular pressure, and it's fairly easy to check. So that's one of the things an ophthalmologist looks for when you get HZO.

Besides cornea damage and the risk of glaucoma, are there any other big threats to the eye from HZO?

The main dangers include cataracts in the lens and inflammation of the eyeball lining, the retina, or the optic nerve. Almost any part of the eye can be affected, which is why careful monitoring and prompt treatment are so important.

What's the main treatment for HZO?

Like other forms of shingles, HZO should be treated with antiviral drugs as early as possible. It's the best way to reduce the risk of eye involvement.

LIVING WITH SHINGLES

Is HZO treated any differently from other kinds of shingles?

The only difference in treatment is a greater willingness to use corticosteroids to fight inflammation. The side effects of steroids make many doctors reluctant to prescribe them, but the potential risks of eye inflammation are so high that some feel that the benefits outweigh the risks.

If my ophthalmologist finds signs of increased pressure in my eye, can anything be done to head off glaucoma?

Glaucoma can usually be controlled with drugs, many applied as eyedrops. Some decrease the production of fluid in the eye; others help the drainage of excess fluid. In extreme cases, surgery may be needed to prevent fluid buildup.

If parts of the eye become severely damaged by HZO, can anything be done to repair them?

Severe damage is uncommon, but if necessary, it can often be repaired by surgery. A badly scarred cornea can be replaced with a human transplant, and a lens with a serious cataract can be replaced with an artificial substitute.

Questions and Answers about Shingles

A neighbor of mine had a very strange kind of shingles. It seemed to be centered in his ear, and it temporarily damaged his hearing. But the really strange thing was that the muscles on the side of his face were paralyzed. What did he have?

Shingles in the facial nerve often affects nearby nerves, causing a group of symptoms called Ramsay Hunt syndrome. The symptoms include earache, rash in or around the ear, loss of taste in part of the tongue, loss of hearing, dizziness, and paralysis of facial muscles. Most of them disappear with the acute infection, but the facial paralysis and hearing loss may linger for some time.

I know that as a rule the chickenpox rash appears over much of the body, while shingles turns up in just one area. Does shingles ever "escape" to other parts of the body?

Shingles is usually confined to a single dermatome. Only rarely does it spread, or disseminate, elsewhere. Disseminated shingles occurs almost entirely in individuals who are severely immunosuppressed. It can be very dangerous, for unlike ordinary shingles, it can affect internal organs, causing pneumonia in the lungs, or inflammation of the brain and its membranes (encephalitis).

The Varicella Vaccine

If you don't ever have chickenpox, does it mean you won't ever get shingles?

If you never have chickenpox, then the varicella-zoster virus that causes it can't become stored in your nerve roots. And if there's no virus in the nerve roots, it can't become reactivated to cause shingles. In short: no chickenpox, no shingles—at least in theory.

Is there really an effective way of preventing chickenpox?

The varicella vaccine (brand name Varivax) effectively prevents most chickenpox. It protects from seventy to ninety percent of those vaccinated against any symptoms at all, and ninety-five percent against a severe attack.

Are there people who would particularly benefit by never catching chickenpox?

180

Questions and Answers about Shingles

Several groups of people would benefit greatly if they never got chickenpox. For example:

- People who didn't have chickenpox during childhood. Infection can occur at any age, and adolescents and adults are likely to get much sicker than children.

- People who are severely immunosuppressed, from hereditary immunodeficiencies, from disease, or from medical treatment. Chickenpox can make them dangerously ill.

- Pregnant women. If they get chickenpox in early pregnancy, their babies may have serious birth defects. If they have it around the time of delivery, their babies may be severely infected.

My son says that he and his wife aren't going to have their children vaccinated against chickenpox because they had it themselves when they were little, and it wasn't serious enough to be worth preventing. Are they right?

Chickenpox is considered a mild disease, at least compared with some other rash diseases. But it

181

makes many children quite miserable, and costs their families much time and inconvenience taking care of them. Even more important, a small but significant number of people have real trouble with chickenpox. Every year, thousands of them have to go to the hospital, and about one hundred die.

What exactly is a vaccine? How does it protect you from a virus?

A vaccine is a chemical substance that is either derived from a particular virus, or else resembles it closely. When it is injected into your body, the look-alike won't cause disease, but it will "fool" your immune system into developing antibodies to the real virus. Thereafter, if you are infected by the virus, the antibodies will attach themselves to it, and will mark it for quick destruction by other parts of your immune system. In short, you are now immune to that virus.

How is the varicella vaccine produced?

The varicella vaccine is a weakened, or attenuated, form of the virus. That is, the virus has been manipulated so it can't multiply and cause disease. But it is enough like the full-strength virus that the immune system will develop antibodies to the virus.

Questions and Answers about Shingles

When and how is the varicella vaccine administered?

The vaccine is customarily given to children from the time they are twelve months old. For those up to twelve years old, only a single shot is needed to give lasting protection. Adolescents and adults are given two shots, spaced four weeks apart.

Aside from preventing chickenpox, does the vaccine have any other benefits?

Even when the vaccine doesn't completely prevent chickenpox, it almost always prevents serious symptoms. Any "breakthrough" infection is likely to be mild, with a lower fever, fewer bumps, and a quicker recovery. The vaccine also protects against the possible complications of chickenpox, such as secondary bacterial infection. Finally, the vaccine may even offer hope to people who have been exposed to the virus but haven't already been vaccinated. If the vaccine is injected within three days of the exposure, infection appears to be prevented.

183

LIVING WITH SHINGLES

Does the vaccine have any significant side effects?

The possible side effects of the vaccine are relatively minor. The most common is inflammation at the injection site, followed by low fever and mild headache. Less common is an outbreak of rash, which may represent a low-level chickenpox infection.

A year ago, our daughter's pediatrician didn't want to vaccinate her for chickenpox, but at our recent visit he recommended it. What changed his mind?

Until quite recently, many pediatricians were hesitant to use the vaccine. They weren't sure its protection would last, and they thought it would be better for children to get the disease and develop immunity, rather than catch it later on. But every year more and more evidence mounts up that the vaccine does give lasting protection, and that the protection can be reinforced with booster shots if necessary. So there's a growing consensus that vaccination of children should be routine.

Is there anybody who shouldn't get the vaccine?

There are some individuals for whom the vaccine isn't recommended. They include:

184

- Those who have an active infectious disease such as tuberculosis.

- Those who are allergic to vaccine components, such as gelatin and the antibiotic neomycin.

- Those who have recently received blood transfusions, or injections of immune globulins.

- Pregnant women. The vaccine hasn't been proved harmless to a developing fetus.

- Those who have weakened immune systems.

Why isn't the vaccine recommended for people who have weak immune systems? Aren't they just the ones who need it most?

The reason is caution. If an individual has a very weak immune system, the vaccine may be unable to stimulate it sufficiently to achieve immunity. Instead, it may make the person even more susceptible to infection.

185

LIVING WITH SHINGLES

But the virus is being tested on such individuals—children with leukemia, for example. So far, the results are promising, and approval for the vaccine has been extended to this group.

How can we be sure that people who get the vaccine not only won't get chickenpox, but won't come down with shingles later on?

It will take decades to prove for sure that the vaccine will prevent shingles as well as chickenpox. But already there's some promising evidence. Children with leukemia often get severe chickenpox, followed by shingles just a few years later. When they're vaccinated, far fewer of them develop either chickenpox or shingles.

I've already had chickenpox. What can the varicella vaccine do for *me*?

The vaccine may prove to be able to reduce shingles in adults who have had chickenpox. One relatively small, short experiment suggests that it can, and much larger studies are now under way. We won't have any results, though, for several years, and even then they may not be conclusive.

186

GLOSSARY

Acetominophen (brand names Tylenol, Datril, Panadol, etc.). Over-the counter analgesic (painkiller) that alters the perception of pain in the central nervous system. Acetominophen has fewer potentially harmful side effects than aspirin and other nonsteroidal anti-inflammatory drugs (NSAIDs).

Acetylsalicylic acid (ASA). Medical name for aspirin. *See also* Nonsteroidal anti-inflammatory drugs.

Acyclovir (brand name Zovirax). Antiviral drug, taken orally (by mouth) or intravenously (by injection). *See also* Antiviral drugs, Famcyclovir, Valaciclovir.

AIDS. Abbreviation for acquired immune deficiency syndrome. *See also* HIV.

LIVING WITH SHINGLES

Allodynia. Neurogenic pain, triggered by some sensation that is not in itself painful, such as a light, moving touch across the skin. Allodynia is more typical of post-herpetic neuralgia (PHN) than of shingles. *See also* Neurogenic pain.

Aluminum acetate (Burow's solution). Astringent solution used in wet dressings or compresses to firm and dry the skin, and to relieve the pain of shingles by drawing out irritants such as prostaglandins.

Amitriptyline (brand names Elavil, Endep). Tricyclic antidepressant drug used to treat post-herpetic neuralgia (PHN). *See also* Antidepressants, Tricyclic antidepressants.

Antibodies. Protein molecules produced by certain white blood cells of the immune system. Antibodies attach themselves to foreign invaders, marking them for destruction by other immune cells. Also known as immune globulins and immunoglobulins. *See also* Varicella-zoster immune globulin.

Anticonvulsants. Drugs mainly used to treat epileptic seizures, but also used to relieve post-herpetic neuralgia (PHN). Anticonvulsants are often prescribed for allodynia, which is thought to be caused by the uncontrolled, abnormal firing of pain-sensing neurons. *See also* Allodynia, Carbamazepine, Gabapentin, Phenytoin.

Antidepressants. Drugs mainly used to relieve psychological depression, but administered in smaller doses to relieve post-herpetic neuralgia (PHN). They apparently enhance the activity of chemical neurotransmitters in spinal nerves that hinder the transmission of pain impulses to the brain.

188

Glossary

See also Amitriptyline, Desipramine, Maprotiline, Neurotransmitters, Nortriptyline, Tricyclic antidepressants.

Antiprurients. Anti-itch medications.

Antiviral drugs. Drugs used to control virus attacks. They do not kill the virus, but stop it from reproducing. Antivirals act selectively upon the virus, and have little or no effect on normal cells. *See also* Famcyclovir, Foscarnet, Valacyclovir.

Aspercreme. Brand name for tolamine salicylate, an anti-itch (antiprurient) medication.

Attenuated virus. Biologically manipulated virus that cannot reproduce well enough to cause disease, used as a vaccine.

Axon. See Neuron.

Bacitracin. Topical antibiotic, applied to the skin to prevent bacterial infection.

Behavioral therapy. Form of psychological treatment sometimes used in the treatment of long-persisting post-herpetic neuralgia (PHN). Behavioral therapy is designed to reduce the effects of pain upon day-to-day behavior, enabling the patient to live a more normal life and to experience pain less intensely.

Ben-Gay. Popular rubefacient topical medication. *See* Rubefacients.

Biofeedback. Electrical amplifier of physical signs of psychological stress, sometimes used in the treatment of post-

LIVING WITH SHINGLES

herpetic neuralgia (PHN) to raise awareness of stress and assist relaxation.

Breakthrough infection. Infection that occurs in someone already vaccinated against it. Breakthrough chickenpox infection, after immunization with the varicella vaccine, is uncommon and tends to be relatively mild.

Burow's solution. *See* Aluminum acetate.

Calamine lotion. Anti-itch (antiprurient) medication, based on zinc oxide and ferric oxide.

Capsaicin (brand names Zostrix, Dolorac, Capzacin). Topical medication used to treat post-herpetic neuralgia (PHN). It is derived from hot peppers, and appears to lower the level of a neurotransmitter that facilitates the passage of pain impulses between neurons (nerve cells). *See also* Neurotransmitters.

Capzacin. Brand name for Capsaicin, a topical medication used to treat post-herpetic neuralgia (PHN). *See* Capsaicin.

Carbamazepine (brand name Tegretol). Anticonvulsant drug used to treat post-herpetic neuralgia (PHN). *See also* Anticonvulsants.

Cataract. Cloudy area in the lens of the eye, which may impair vision. Cataracts may result from inflammation of the lens by herpes zoster ophthalmicus. *See also* Herpes zoster ophthalmicus.

Causalgia. Disease that produces burning neurogenic pain in the area of a nerve-damaging injury, such as a severe wound. *See* Neurogenic pain.

190

Glossary

Chemotherapy. Medical treatment with drugs that kill cancer cells, but that often suppress the immune system as well.

Chickenpox. Usually mild, extremely contagious rash disease caused by the varicella-zoster virus. Infection results in lasting immunity to chickenpox, but virus surviving in one or more sensory nerve roots may later reactivate, causing shingles.

Choroid. Inner lining of the eyeball, which may be inflamed and damaged by herpes zoster ophthalmicus. *See also* Herpes zoster ophthalmicus.

Cingulum. Latin word from which the name shingles is derived. Cingulum means "belt," referring to the typical location of the shingles rash, in a horizontal band around one side of the chest or abdomen. *See also* Zoster.

Codeine. Narcotic (opioid) occasionally used to relieve the pain of shingles. *See also* Narcotics.

Cognitive psychotherapy. Type of psychotherapy sometimes used in the treatment of long-persisting post-herpetic neuralgia (PHN). Therapy aims to reconstruct mental attitudes toward pain to encourage coping and healing rather than emotional suffering.

Conjunctivitis. Inflammation of the conjunctiva, a transparent mucous membrane that protects the white of the eye. Conjunctivitis is a common complication of herpes zoster ophthalmicus. *See also* Herpes zoster ophthalmicus.

Controlled breathing. Timed sequence of inhalations and exhalations, used to manage stress through physical relaxation.

Corticosteroids. Hormones produced in the outer layer (cortex) of the adrenal glands, or drugs derived from or resembling these hormones. Corticosteroids are often simply called steroids. They are controversial in the treatment of shingles, for although they relieve inflammation, they have several potentially harmful side effects, including the suppression of the immune system.

Counterirritation. Using mildly irritating sensations to stimulate the central nervous system to inhibit the transmission of more painful sensations. Counterirritants include vigorous massage, rubefacient liniments such as oil of wintergreen (Ben-Gay), and possibly transcutaneous electrical nerve stimulation (TENS). *See also* Rubefacients, Transcutaneous electrical nerve stimulation.

Cranial nerves. Nerves that connect to the brainstem within the skull (the cranium), and that mainly serve the head and neck. *See also* Facial nerve, Trigeminal nerve.

Cytomegalovirus. Virus that causes a disease with usually mild, flu-like symptoms. If contracted during pregnancy, however, cytomegalovirus can cause birth defects in the baby.

Dendrites. See Neuron.

Depakene. Brand name of valproic acid, an anticonvulsant drug used to treat post-herpetic neuralgia (PHN). *See also* Anticonvulsants.

Dermatologist. A physician (M.D.) specializing in the treatment of skin disorders.

Dermatome. Body segment (literally, a "skin slice"), served by one sensory nerve or nerve branch. Shingles is usually confined to a single dermatome.

Desipramine. Tricyclic antidepressant drug used to treat post-herpetic neuralgia (PHN). *See also* Antidepressants, Tricyclic antidepressants.

Diazepam (brand name Valium). Drug used to relieve dizziness caused by shingles of the facial nerve. *See also* Ramsay Hunt syndrome.

Diflusinal (brand name Dolobid). Prescription nonsteroidal anti-inflammatory drug (NSAID).

Dilantin. Brand name of phenytoin, an anticonvulsant drug used to treat post-herpetic neuralgia (PHN). *See also* Anticonvulsants.

DNA (deoxyribonucleic acid). Long, twisted, ladderlike molecule known as the double helix, which carries the genetic code for reproduction. Living cells usually contain several strands of DNA, in the form of chromosomes. The varicella-zoster virus contains a single DNA molecule, wrapped in a protective coating of protein.

Dolobid. Brand name of diflusinal, a prescription nonsteroidal anti-inflammatory drug (NSAID).

Dolorac. Brand name for capsaicin, a topical medication used to treat post-herpetic neuralgia (PHN). *See* Capsaicin.

Dorsal ganglia. Enlarged portions of sensory nerve roots, containing the cell bodies of the sensory neurons. The ganglia are located toward the back of the spinal cord (*dorsal* means "back") near the points where they connect with the central nerves. *See also* Ventral roots.

Double blind. Condition required of controlled clinical tests, to eliminate bias and reinforce reliability of results. Subjects are given either the test substance or a lookalike "dummy," and neither the subjects nor those giving the substances know which is which.

Doxepin. (brand name Zonalon). Anti-itch (antiprurient) medication.

Elavil. Brand name of a tricyclic antidepressant drug used to treat post-herpetic neuralgia (PHN). *See also* Antidepressants, Tricyclic antidepressants.

Encephalitis. Inflammation of the brain and its surrounding membranes, occasionally caused by severe chickenpox or disseminated shingles.

Endep. Brand name of a tricyclic antidepressant drug used to treat post-herpetic neuralgia (PHN). *See also* Antidepressants, Tricyclic antidepressants.

Epstein-Barr virus. Virus that causes mononucleosis.

Facial nerve. Cranial nerve that registers pain sensations on the side of the face, taste sensations from half of the tongue, and hearing and balance sensations from the ear. A nearby motor nerve controls facial expressions. Shingles of the facial nerve may affect both sensory and motor functions, a condition known as Ramsay Hunt syndrome. *See also* Cranial nerves.

Glossary

Famcyclovir (brand name Famvir). Antiviral prodrug, taken orally (by mouth). Prodrugs are chemically converted to active form during absorption into the body. *See also* Acyclovir, Antiviral drugs, Valaciclovir.

Feldene. Brand name of piroxicam, a prescription non-steroidal anti-inflammatory drug (NSAID).

Foscarnet (brand name Foscavir). Antiviral drug, which is stronger than those customarily used to treat shingles, but more likely to cause harmful side effects—kidney damage in particular. *See also* Antiviral drugs.

Gabapentin (brand name Neurontin). Anticonvulsant drug used to treat post-herpetic neuralgia (PHN). *See also* Anticonvulsants.

Glaucoma. Vision-threatening disease caused by excessive pressure within the eyeball. It sometimes results from the inflammation of herpes zoster ophthalmicus. *See also* Herpes zoster ophthalmicus.

Guided imagery. Technique for stress management, using imagination to distract attention away from unpleasant thoughts, feelings, and sensations, including the perception of pain.

Herpes simplex, type 1. Virus that causes oral herpes, or cold sores.

Herpes simplex, type 2. Virus that causes genital herpes.

Herpes zoster opthalmicus (HZO). Shingles that originates in the upper, or ophthalmic, branch of the trigeminal nerve of the face. It produces a rash in the area between the forehead and the end of the nose, and often infects the eye. *See also* Trigeminal nerve.

Herpesviruses. A related group of viruses that include, in addition to varicella-zoster virus, cytomegalovirus, Epstein-Barr virus, and herpes simplex viruses type 1 and type 2.

HIV. Abbreviation for human immunovirus, a virus that attacks the human immune system and causes AIDS (acquired immune deficiency syndrome).

Hutchinson's sign. Patch of rash near the tip of the nose. It is an early symptom of herpes zoster ophthalmicus, and is considered evidence that the eye will eventually be affected. *See also* Herpes zoster ophthalmicus.

Hypnosis. Artificially induced state of consciousness (trance) in which the subject becomes strongly susceptible to suggestion. Hypnotism is sometimes used in the treatment of post-herpetic neuralgia (PHN) to distract attention from the perception of pain, through such techniques as sensory substitution. *See also* Sensory substitution.

HZO. Abbreviation of herpes zoster ophthalmicus.

Ibuprofen (brand names Advil, Motrin, Nuprin, etc.). Widely used over-the-counter nonsteroidal anti-inflammatory drug (NSAID).

Immune memory. Ability of the immune system to recognize a specific invader, such as a virus, after a first infection.

Immune system. System composed mainly of white blood cells and their products, which identifies and attacks foreign invaders of the body, such as viruses, bacteria, and funguses.

Immunoglobulins. See Antibodies.

Immunosuppressed. Lacking the protection of a normal immune system, as the result of aging, disease, genetic defect, drugs, or radiation.

Indomethacin (brand name Indocin). Prescription non-steroidal anti-inflammatory drug (NSAID).

Iritis. Inflammation of the iris of the eye, a muscular ring that controls the amount of light passing through the pupil. Severe iritis, caused by herpes zoster ophthalmicus, may cause lasting damage to the eye, and can also lead to the vision-threatening disorder glaucoma. *See also* Glaucoma, Herpes zoster ophthalmicus.

Keratitis. Inflammation of the cornea, a transparent window of tissue in the front of the eye. Keratitis caused by herpes zoster ophthalmicus may lead to ulceration or scarring that impairs vision. *See also* Herpes zoster ophthalmicus.

Lidocaine. Topical anesthetic, applied to the skin for temporary relief of pain.

Malaise. Vague, unspecific sensation of being unwell, which is sometimes a preliminary symptom of shingles.

Maprotiline. Antidepressant drug used to treat post-herpetic neuralgia (PHN). *See also* Antidepressants.

LIVING WITH SHINGLES

Meditation. Technique for stress management, which distracts attention away from everyday thoughts, feelings, and sensations, including the perception of pain.

Menthol. Rubefacient topical medication. *See* Rubefacients.

Meperidine (brand name Demerol). Narcotic (opioid) occasionally used to relieve the pain of post-herpetic neuralgia. *See also* Narcotics.

Motor nerves. Nerves carrying impulses from the central nervous system (brain and spinal cord) to control the movements of muscles. *See also* Sensory nerves, Ventral roots.

Naproxen (brand name Naprocyn). Prescription nonsteroidal anti-inflammatory drug (NSAID).

Narcotics (opioids). Pain-relieving drugs either derived from or chemically similar to opium. They inhibit the transmission of pain sensations among nerve cells. Those used to treat shingles are relatively mild forms such as codeine or propoxyphene (Darvon), alone or in combination with other drugs. *See also* Meperidine, Oxycodone, Propoxyphene.

Nerve blocks. Techniques to stop the passage of pain sensations through nerves, used occasionally in the treatment of shingles and post-herpetic neuralgia (PHN). Temporary blocks are achieved with injections of local anesthetic. Longer lasting blocks require severing the nerve by surgery, chemicals, heat, or cold. Blocks may be performed upon sensory nerves, or upon the sympathetic nerves that control automatic body functions. Even long-term blocks produce only temporary relief.

198

Glossary

Neurogenic pain. Burning or stabbing pain produced by damage or malfunction within neurons (nerve cells). Neurogenic pain is typical not only of shingles, but also of conditions such as trigeminal neuralgia, causalgia, stump pain, and phantom limb pain. *See also* Allodynia, Phantom limb pain, Stump pain, Trigeminal neuralgia.

Neuron. Nerve cell. Each neuron of a sensory nerve has a cell body, containing the cell nucleus, near one end, at the nerve root. From the cell body extends a tubelike axon, ending in branchlike dendrites that receive sensory impulses from the skin and other organs.

Neurontin. Brand name of gabapentin, an anticonvulsant drug used to treat post-herpetic neuralgia (PHN). *See also* Anticonvulsants.

Neurotransmitters. Chemicals generated by neurons (nerve cells) that pass impulses to other neurons. Several of the drugs used to treat shingles and post-herpetic neuralgia (PHN) either strengthen or inhibit natural neurotransmitters of the nervous system.

NMDA Blockers. Drugs being tried experimentally in the treatment of post-herpetic neuralgia (PHN). They block the input ends of pain-sensing neurons (nerve cells), preventing them from transmitting impulses to the brain.

Nonsteroidal anti-inflammatory drugs (NSAIDs). Drugs such as aspirin and ibuprofen, which relieve the swelling and pain of inflammation. NSAIDs block the production of chemicals called prostaglandins, generated by damaged cells. NSAIDs also affect the perception of pain in the central nervous system.

199

Nortriptyline. Tricyclic antidepressant drug used to treat post-herpetic neuralgia (PHN). *See also* Antidepressants, Tricyclic antidepressants.

Oil of wintergreen. Rubefacient topical medication. *See* Rubefacients.

Ophthalmologist. A physician (M.D.) specializing in treatment of the eyes.

Opioids. Medical name for narcotics.

Optic nerve. Nerve carrying visual information from the retina of the eye to the brain. The optic nerve can be directly inflamed and damaged by herpes zoster ophthalmicus, or indirectly by glaucoma resulting from the viral infection. *See also* Glaucoma, Herpes zoster ophthalmicus.

Oxycodone (brand names Percocet, Percodan). Narcotic (opioid) occasionally used to relieve the pain of post-herpetic neuralgia. *See also* Narcotics.

Pain clinics. Facilities offering comprehensive, multifaceted treatment of painful disorders such as post-herpetic neuralgia (PHN). Pain clinics employ a team of specialists that may include a neurologist, an anesthesiologist, a physical therapist, and a psychologist, among others.

Papules. Small bumps that form the first stage of the shingles rash. *See also* Pustules, Vesicles.

Pepcid. Antiulcer and antiheartburn drug, which reduces the production of stomach acid and may counteract the irritation of the stomach lining by nonsteroidal anti-inflammatory drugs (NSAIDs). *See also* Nonsteroidal anti-inflammatory drugs.

Percocet, Percodan. Brand names of oxycodone, a narcotic (opioid) occasionally used to relieve the pain of post-herpetic neuralgia. *See also* Narcotics.

Phantom limb pain. Neurogenic pain that seems to originate in a limb that has been amputated. *See* Neurogenic pain.

Phenytoin (brand name Dilantin). Anticonvulsant drug used to treat post-herpetic neuralgia (PHN). *See also* Anticonvulsants.

PHN. Abbreviation for post-herpetic neuralgia.

Piroxicam (brand name Feldene). Prescription nonsteroidal anti-inflammatory drug (NSAID).

Pneumonia. Inflammation of the lungs, occasionally caused by severe chickenpox or disseminated shingles.

Post-herpetic neuralgia (PHN). Pain that persists or recurs long after the shingles rash has healed. Post-herpetic neuralgia is usually defined as pain experienced more than five weeks past the first appearance of the rash.

Pramoxine. Topical anesthetic, applied to the skin for temporary relief of pain.

Prednisone. Corticosteroid drug, sometimes used to treat shingles. *See* Corticosteroids.

Progressive relaxation. Sequence of exercises used for stress management, in which muscle groups are relaxed one at a time, from the feet to the head.

Propoxyphene (brand name Darvon). Narcotic (opioid) occasionally used to relieve shingles pain. *See also* Narcotics.

Prostaglandins. Chemicals produced by damaged cells, which stimulate pain-sensing nerves. *See* Nonsteroidal anti-inflammatory drugs.

Pustules. Blisters filled with cloudy pus, which form the third stage of the shingles rash. *See also* Papules, Vesicles.

Ramsay Hunt syndrome. Group of symptoms caused by shingles of the facial nerve, which may include rash in and around the ear, severe earache, hearing loss, dizziness, nausea, partial taste loss, and facial muscle paralysis. *See also* Facial nerve.

Retina. "Screen" at the back of the eye that receives visual images projected through the lens and converts them into sensory impulses to be transmitted through the optic nerve to the brain. The retina can be inflamed and damaged by herpes zoster ophthalmicus. *See also* Herpes zoster ophthalmicus.

Rubefacients. "Red-making" liniments and ointments that dilate the blood vessels, causing the skin to flush and feel warm, and also act as counterirritants to the transmission of pain sensations. *See also* Counterirritation.

Sclera. White of the eye, and other outer layers of the eyeball, which may be inflamed by Herpes zoster ophthalmicus. *See also* Herpes zoster ophthalmicus.

Glossary

Sensory nerves. Nerves carrying sensory impulses from the skin and other organs to the central nervous system (spinal cord and brain). *See also* Motor nerves, Neuron.

Sensory substitution. Technique for stress management, using imagination to substitute a nonpainful sensation, such as coolness or mild prickling, for a painful one. *See also* Hypnosis.

Silver sulfadiazine. Topical antibacterial, applied to the skin to prevent bacterial infection.

Stump pain. Neurogenic pain at the site of an amputation. *See* Neurogenic pain.

Tagamet. Antiulcer and antiheartburn drug, which reduces the production of stomach acid and may counteract the irritation of the stomach lining by nonsteroidal anti-inflammatory drugs (NSAIDs). *See also* Nonsteroidal anti-inflammatory drugs.

Tegretol. Brand name of carbamazepine, an anticonvulsant drug used to treat post-herpetic neuralgia (PHN). *See also* Anticonvulsants.

Temporal arteritis. Inflammation of a blood vessel in the temple, causing pain sometimes mistaken for that of herpes zoster ophthalmicus. *See also* Herpes zoster ophthalmicus.

TENS. See Transcutaneous electrical nerve stimulation.

Tolamine salicylate (brand name Aspercreme). Anti-itch (antiprurient) medication.

LIVING WITH SHINGLES

Topical anesthetics. Medications applied to the skin, which not only relieve pain but blunt all sensations, producing temporary numbness.

Topical antibiotics and antibacterials. Medications applied to the skin to prevent bacterial infection.

Topical medications. Lotions, creams, ointments, etc., applied to the skin in order to relieve pain or itching, prevent infection, etc.

Transcutaneous electrical nerve stimulation (TENS). Machine that passes mild pulses of electrical current through areas of the skin. TENS is thought to relieve pain by counterirritation. *See also* Counterirritation.

Triamcinolone. Corticosteroid drug, sometimes used to treat shingles. *See also* Corticosteroids.

Tricyclic antidepressants. Class of antidepressant drugs, uniquely effective in the treatment of post-herpetic neuralgia (PHN). *See also* Antidepressants.

Trigeminal nerve. Cranial nerve with three branches (trigeminal means "triplet"), which serves one side of the face. *See also* Cranial nerves, Herpes zoster ophthalmicus.

Trigeminal neuralgia. Inflammation of the trigeminal nerve that causes spasms of stabbing neurogenic pain in the face. It is sometimes mistaken for herpes zoster ophthalmicus. *See also* Herpes zoster ophthalmicus, Neurogenic pain, Trigeminal nerve.

Valacyclovir (brand name Valtrex). Prodrug, taken orally (by mouth). Prodrugs are chemically converted to active

204

Glossary

form during absorption into the body. *See also* Acyclovir, Antiviral drugs, Famcyclovir.

Valium. Brand name of diazepam, drug used to relieve dizziness caused by shingles of the facial nerve. *See also* Ramsay Hunt syndrome.

Valproic acid (brand name Depakene). Anticonvulsant drug used to treat post-herpetic neuralgia (PHN). *See also* Anticonvulsants.

Varicella. Medical name for chickenpox.

Varicella-zoster immune globulin (VZIG). Concentrate of anti-bodies to varicella-zoster virus, which can be injected into individuals who have recently been exposed to chickenpox and need extra protection against the virus. *See also* Antibodies.

Varicella-zoster virus. Virus of the herpes group, which causes both chickenpox (varicella) and zoster (shingles). *See also* Herpesviruses.

Varivax. Brand name of varicella vaccine.

Ventral roots. Roots of the motor nerves, which connect to the spinal cord toward its front side. *See also* Dorsal ganglia, Motor nerves.

Vesicles. Small, fluid-filled blisters that form the second stage of the shingles rash. *See also* Papules, Pustules.

Virions. Individual particles of virus. *See* Virus.

LIVING WITH SHINGLES

Virus. Very small microorganism, composed of a single piece of either DNA or RNA, surrounded by a protective coating of protein. Reproduces by invading the nucleus of a living cell and taking over its genetic machinery to produce more virus.

VZV. Abbreviation for varicella-zoster virus.

Zonalon. Brand name for doxepin, an anti-itch (antipruri-ent) medication.

Zoster. Medical name for shingles, from a Greek word meaning "belt," and referring to the typical location of the shingles rash, in a horizontal band around one side of the chest or abdomen. *See also* Cingulum.

Zostrix. Brand name for capsaicin, a topical medication used to treat post-herpetic neuralgia (PHN). *See* Capsaicin.

Zovirax. Brand name for acyclovir. *See* Antiviral drugs.

HELPFUL SOURCES

The following organizations can be helpful in providing you with information and often in recommending a physician or other health care professional. Many can also provide you with free relevant reading material and/or a catalog of booklets, books, and tapes for purchase.

Academy for Guided Imagery
P.O. Box 2070
Mill Valley, CA 94942
(800) 726-2070
http://www.healthy.net/agi

American Academy of Dermatology
P.O. Box 4014
Schaumburg, IL 60168-4014
(847) 330-0230
http://www.aad.org

LIVING WITH SHINGLES

American Academy of Family Physicians
8880 Ward Parkway
Kansas City, MO 64114
(816) 333-9700
(800) 274-2237
http://www.aafp.org

American Academy of Neurology
1080 Montreal Avenue
St. Paul, MN 55116
(612) 695-1940
(800) 879-1960
http://www.aan.com

American Academy of Ophthalmology
P.O. Box 7424
San Francisco, CA 94120-7424
(415) 561-8500
http://www.eyenet.org

American Academy of Pediatrics
141 Northwest Point Blvd.
Elk Grove Village, IL 60007-1098
(847) 228-5005
(800) 336-5475
http://www.aap.org

American Chronic Pain Association (ACPA)
P.O. Box 850
Rocklin, CA 95677-0850
(916) 632-0922
http://www/theacpa.org

Helpful Sources

American Pain Society
4700 West Lake Avenue
Glenview, IL 60025
(847) 375-4715
http://www.ampainsoc.org/

American Psychiatric Association
1400 K Street, NW
Washington, DC 20005
(202) 682-6000
http://www/psych.org

American Psychological Association
750 First Street, NE
Washington, DC 20002-4242
(202) 336-5500
(800) 374-2721
http://www.apa.org

**Association for Applied
Psychophysiology and Biofeedback**
10200 West 44th Avenue
Suite 304
Wheat Ridge, CO 80333
(303) 422-8436
(800) 477-8892
http://www.aapb.org

LIVING WITH SHINGLES

National Association of Social Workers
750 First Street, NE
Suite 700
Washington, DC 20002-4241
(203) 408-8600
(800) 638-8799
http://www.naswdc.org

VZV Research Foundation
40 East 72nd Street
New York, NY 10021
(212) 472-3181

INDEX

LIVING WITH SHINGLES

Index

Gabapentin, 83
Glaucoma, 107, 112, 176-177, 178
Guided imagery, 64-65

Heart disease, 84
Herpes, 27-28, 32, 33, 149, 152
Herpes zoster opthalmicus. *See*
    HZO
High blood pressure, 84
Hutchinson's sign, 104, 174
Hypnosis, 92, 171
HZO. *See also* Eyes
    anecdotes about patients with,
        101-102, 119-120
    and antibiotics, 110
    and antiviral drugs, 109-110,
        177
    and bacterial infection, 107,
        111, 176
    and corticosteroids, 110, 178
    and Hutchinson's sign, 104, 174
    and NSAIDs, 110
    and opioids, 110
    as possible shingles complica-
        tion, 121, 174
    and potential damage to eye,
        105-109, 175-177
    symptoms of, 104-105
    treatment of, 109-112, 177-178

Ibuprofen, 49, 79, 110, 157
Immune system, 29-30, 149-150
Immunoglobulins. *See* Antibodies
Immunosuppressed, 15, 16, 104,
    116, 117, 126, 135, 141-
    142, 179, 185-186
Indocin, 50, 79
Indomethacin, 50, 79
Inflammation, 49
Insomnia, 76, 168
Iritis, 107-108

Jenner, Edward, 36

Journal of the American Medical
    Association, 132

Keratitis, 106-107, 176
Kidney damage, 47, 51, 52

LaRussa, Philip S., 132
Lens of eye, 108
Leukemia, 135, 136, 186
Lidocaine, 59, 86, 161
Liniments, 164
Liver damage, 52
Loss of appetite, 76, 168
Lotions, 59
Lubricating drops, 111
Lupus, 29, 142

MacDonald, Susan, 8, 23-24, 40, 68
Maprotiline, 81
Massaging, 66
Mechanically assisted relaxation,
    91-92, 171
Meditation, 63-64, 162-163
Meningitis, 19
Mental distraction, 162-163
Menthol, 58, 67, 87
Meperidine, 55
Merck, 128
Mononucleosis, 27
Motrin, 49
Multiple sclerosis, 29
Muscle weakness, 19
Muscles controlling eye move-
    ment, 108-109

Naprocyn, 50, 79
Naproxen, 50, 79
Narcotics. *See* Opioids
Negative pain behavior, 94
Nerve blocks, 95-97, 172
Nervous system, disorders of, 11-12
Neurogenic pain, 11-12
Neurotransmitters, 81, 87

LIVING WITH SHINGLES

214

Index

Piroxicam, 50
Pneumonia, 19, 117-118, 121, 179
Polio, 26, 36
Post-herpetic neuralgia. *See* PHN
Pramoxine, 59, 86, 161
Prednisone, 55
Prilocaine, 161
Progressive relaxation, 61-63, 162
Propoxyphene, 55, 159
Prostaglandins, 50, 55, 58
Prozac, 82
Psychological stress, 161
Psychotherapy, 172
Ptosis, 105

Rabies, 26, 36
Radiation treatment, 16
Ramsay Hunt syndrome, 113-114, 121, 179
Rashes, 18, 104, 143, 174
Recurrence of shingles, 116, 121
Red-making. *See* Rubefacients
Relaxation, 60-64, 90
Retina, 108, 177
Rheumatoid arthritis, 29
RNA, 25, 148
Rubbing alcohol, 59
Rubefacient liniments, 66-67
Rubefacients liniments, 87-88

Scarring, 115, 121
Sclera, 106, 176
Sensory nerve blocks, 95-96
Sensory nerve damage, 33, 77
Sensory substitution, 65, 163
Sertraline, 82
Shapiro, Eugene, 132
Shingles
    and acetaminophen, 48, 51-52, 157
    anecdotes about patients with, 7-9, 23-24, 39-41, 68-69
    and antibiotics, 40, 59
    and antiviral drugs, 42, 44-47, 154, 155, 156
    and bacterial infection, 40, 57, 59, 127
    and Chickenpox, 13-14, 23-24, 32-33, 143, 180
    and corticosteroids, 48, 55-56, 58, 157
    course of, 17-19
    disseminated, 117-118, 121, 179
    and the face, 113-114, 121, 174, 179
    high-risk groups, 15
    and HZO, 121, 144
    identification of, 143-144
    and the immunosuppressed, 15, 16, 116, 117, 126, 141-142, 179
    and infection of/by another, 23-24, 147-148, 151
    location of, on body, 140
    and necessity of early treatment, 44
    and nerve cells, 13-14
    and NSAIDs, 48, 49-51
    and opioids, 48, 52-55, 157
    origin of name, 10
    pain of, 12
    and pain relievers, 157-159
    and palliative remedies, 42
    and PHN, 10, 18-19, 69, 77, 121, 146, 165, 167
    possible complications from, 101-122, 121-122
    and Ramsay Hunt Syndrome, 113-114, 121, 179
    and rashes, 18, 143, 144-145
    recurrence of, 116, 146
    severity of, 146
    and stress, 60-65, 161-162
    symptoms of, 10, 17-19, 45-46, 139, 144
    and TENS, 67, 164